Compassionate
CAREGIVING

Practical Help and Spiritual Encouragement

Compassionate
CAREGIVING

Practical Help and Spiritual Encouragement

Lois D. KNUTSON

BETHANYHOUSE

Minneapolis, Minnesota

Published by Bethany House Publishers
11400 Hampshire Avenue South
Bloomington, Minnesota 55438

Bethany House Publishers is a division of
Baker Publishing Group, Grand Rapids, Michigan.

Printed in the United States of America

Library of Congress Cataloging-in-Publication Data

Knutson, Lois D.
    Compassionate caregiving : practical help and spiritual encouragement / Lois Knutson.
      p.   cm.
    Summary: "Practical help, encouragement, and spiritual direction for family members or friends who are caregivers for their elderly loved ones"—Provided by publisher.
    Includes bibliographical references.
    ISBN-13: 978-0-7642-0371-8 (pbk.)
    ISBN-10: 0-7642-0371-1 (pbk.)
    1. Caregivers.   2. Older people—Care.   3. Care of the sick—Psychological aspects.   4. Terminal care.   5. Consumer education.   I. Title.
    RC108.K58   2007
    616'.029—dc22

                                                2007002600

To My Mother,
Olive Ione (Bolstad) Knutson

It is a pleasure and a blessing
to honor and help you.

You are my inspiration.

I love you, Mom!

LOIS D. KNUTSON, MDiv, is a caregiver for her mother and has been a pastor for twenty-five years. She has also been a hospital chaplain at the Mayo Clinic hospitals. She completed the Geriatric Pastoral Care Institute at Luther Seminary in St. Paul, Minnesota, and is a nationally sought-after speaker on older adult ministry. Lois was featured in the PBS documentary *And Thou Shalt Honor,* which covered the subject of caregiving. She lives in the upper Midwest. She is available for speaking engagements and can be contacted by e-mail at kairostpt@yahoo.com.

CONTENTS

Introduction

I was visiting a member of my congregation who was in the Intensive Care Unit at Stanford Medical Center in northern California, when I experienced a feeling of personal dread. Something told me to telephone my mother, who lives alone in a small town in southern Minnesota. With haste I excused myself from my parishioner and his family to make the call.

Mom's telephone rang and rang—and it rang some more. In fact, it rang so long that my connection was cut off. I telephoned a second time and the same thing happened. I was very worried about Mom, who is usually at home. I telephoned a third time; and just when I thought I would be disconnected again, I heard a faint voice struggle to say, "Hello." It was my mother!

My sense of dread had been accurate. Mom very slowly told me—speaking one word at a time with pauses in between words—that she was lying on the floor of her small bathroom and was in such excruciating pain that she could not get up. Thankfully, she had just begun to use the cordless telephone that I had given her.

"I can't hold the phone," my mother stated weakly.

"Try, Mom—you have to try."

"I—I—I can't get up from the floor. I can't get back to my bedroom."

"What are your symptoms, Mom? What's going on? Are you injured?"

"It's my stomach—ooh—it hurts. . . ."

"I'm going to get you help, Mom. I love you. I have to hang up now so I can make another phone call. I love you."

I knew that my mother would not want me to dial 9-1-1 unless it was a life and death situation, but this came close. I immediately telephoned my brother's workplace, a few miles away from Mom's house, and told the receptionist, "I'm calling from California. This is an emergency! I need to talk to my brother! Our mother is very ill and needs immediate help! Hurry!"

I could not sleep on that red-eye flight home to Minnesota. All I could think of was the possibility of Mom's dying. I had spoken with her surgeon before I boarded the plane. He matter-of-factly said, "It's probably a strangulated hernia. Your mother may not survive. It's very serious." In the wee hours of the morning on that airplane, I said to myself, "Oh, how I love my mother. I don't know how I would survive if she died." I tried to hide the tears running down my cheeks when the flight attendant periodically walked down the aisle. I prayed without ceasing for Mom. I was soooo sad.

Thankfully, Mom made it through the surgery and is still living twelve years later. This emotionally painful experience was a wake-up call for me, however. As I returned to California, I realized that Mom was growing older and had begun to need help with the activities of daily life. Who would help her? *Me*. There was no one else. My brother was involved with his own family. I am single. I had a decision to make. Should I move back to Minnesota?

I prayed about my decision, but I had two primary personal concerns. First, I loved the California climate. I had never liked Midwestern winters. Second, I knew that if I relocated I would be leaving a position of employment without having another one to replace it. I also knew that when I found a new job, it would probably be at a reduced income. My love for Mom, however, was greater than these considerations, so I decided to move.

After the decision was made, I was at peace, knowing that I would be more readily available to help Mom, who in years past had also made personal sacrifices caring for her aging mother.

I had a difficult choice to make. Not all caregivers can make the decision I did. Each caregiver's situation is different.

God blessed me throughout the relocation process. After only three months of living in Minnesota, God called me to a position that was a four-hour drive (eight hours round trip) from Mom's home. This was the same amount of driving time as had previously been my flight time. Over the course of seven years, I put over 110,000 miles on my car.

Now that I have a job only a seventy-five-minute drive away, I can more easily be Mom's long-distance primary caregiver. I spend nearly every day off with Mom, accompanying her to appointments, taking her grocery shopping, doing chores around the house, drinking coffee with her, and enjoying her company. Throughout the other days of the week, I help her with paper work (from afar), telephone her every morning and evening, strive to find new ways of making her daily life easier, and pray for her.

Yes, I know what it is to be a family caregiver. While it is always an honor and blessing to care for Mom, who in addition to the somewhat usual challenges of the aging process also suffers from scoliosis (a curvature of the spine) and fibromyalgia (a nearly constant pain condition exacerbated by changes in weather and stress), sometimes it is also disheartening and exhausting.

I also know what it is to be a professional caregiver. As an ordained minister, I have served in six congregations, a large, highly respected medical center, two other large hospitals, and a nursing home. I have also done post-graduate study in geriatric pastoral care. These professional caregiving experiences and advanced study opportunities resulted in my first book, *Understanding the Senior Adult: A Tool for Wholistic Ministry* (published by The Alban Institute). Based upon additional study and personal and professional experience, I have written this book to encourage you as you care for your loved one—because I know how heavily the responsibilities of caregiving weigh upon the heart of the one who provides care.

As you apply the tips in this book, you will be encouraged not to give up or give in to feelings of depression or impatient behavior with your care recipient for three reasons. First, you will view your caregiving role as a spiritual calling from God, based upon Luke 10:27: " 'Love the Lord your God with all your heart and with all your soul and with all your strength and with all your mind'; and 'Love your neighbor as yourself.' " Second, you will help yourself as you follow the spiritual and psychological nurturing suggestions in this book. And third, you will experience less helplessness and confusion as you apply the hands-on caregiving helps to your situation.

Some of the questions I will seek to answer in this book are the following:

- How do I keep my spirit up when my care recipient makes impossible demands?

- Are there stages to caregiving? If so, which one am I in?

- How do I interview a home health care agency and its staff and impress upon them the need for Christian compassion and tenderness?

- How do we conduct a family conference so that tempers do not flare up?

- When and how do I approach my loved one about the need to relocate to an assisted-living facility or nursing home? How do we select the appropriate facility?

- What words do I use when saying my final good-byes to my loved one who is dying and will soon meet our Lord face-to-face?

Don't rush through *Compassionate Caregiving*. Read the chapters that apply to you now and scan the rest so that you are aware of how other parts might help you in the future. Carry the book with you if you do not live with your care recipient. Don't put it on a shelf and think you have finished it. Return to it often for spiritual encouragement and practical tips. The book might even serve as a guide when we ourselves become *care recipients*.

I pray that my book will lift your spirit and fill you with hope and peace as you care for your loved one. God bless you—and take heart. God loves you. Caregiving is an important and meaningful spiritual calling.

Chapter One
Caregiving Is a Spiritual Calling

I did not realize it at the time, but when I first began caring for Mom after moving back to Minnesota, my approach to caregiving was similar to that of a fire fighter. A medical, psychological, socio-economic, or family crisis developed and I tried to "put it out" in the most effective way possible. As the number of crises increased, at times I became discouraged and knew that I needed something deeper to keep me going—in addition to my love for Mom.

Discouragement is a daily temptation when caring for a spouse, parent, or friend who needs extra help. Whether you are a first-time caregiver or experienced caregiver, live with (or near) your care recipient or provide long-distance care, are in the work force or have quit your job to be a caregiver, sometimes your experience is so stressful in body, mind, and spirit that you feel as if you can't do it any longer. Please don't give up. I have written this book to help you!

You may ask, "How do I *not* give in to discouragement?" I've found that my *perspective* on caregiving makes a big difference. View your caregiving as a spiritual experience in which you follow Jesus' threefold calling for your life:

"Love the Lord your *God* with all your heart and with all your soul and with all your strength and with all your mind"; and, "Love your *neighbor* as *yourself*" (Luke 10:27, emphasis added).

As we follow this sacred calling—to love God, neighbor, and self—God's peace tenderly boosts our spirit so that we do not give up, even when we are faced with the most stressful caregiving challenges.

As you reflect on this spiritual calling throughout the day, you will be pleasantly amazed at what a difference your spiritual focus makes! Your calling will help you to see beyond daily tasks and instead realize that you are following God's will for your life as a caregiver. Here's how it works.

LOVE GOD

The first part of your threefold calling is to love God ("Love the Lord your God . . ."), who created you in his image and proclaimed you to be "very good" (Genesis 1:31). God cares about you and assures you that you are precious to him. Take heart, God honors you and loves you (Isaiah 43:4).

God understands all that you experience as a caregiver. He knows that you are making personal sacrifices that people around you do not always understand, acknowledge, or appreciate. He recognizes that being a caregiver is difficult. He is pleased that you have accepted your caregiving role, and he promises to take care of you. You are God's care recipient just as your loved one is. God loves you both.

As you remember God's love for you, love God in return—with all your heart, soul, strength, and mind—and confidently cling to him every day. Remember, it is part of your spiritual calling to love God.

LOVE YOUR CARE RECIPIENT

The second part of your calling is to love your care recipient ("Love your *neighbor* as yourself"). Your care recipient is also your neighbor, because "a neighbor is someone who is near you and a person with whom you have something to do."[1] Your loved one is near and dear to you, if not geographically, in heart and spirit.

Your care recipient is important to God, just as you are. She was created in God's image, just as you were. Both of you belong to God. God loves your care recipient with her imperfections, just as God loves you with yours. Your loved one's value does not diminish in God's eyes because, for example, her mobility is not as agile as in past years or her mind is not as alert—just as your value to God does not diminish because of your limitations in life. Love your care recipient with the same love that God has for both of you.

Loving your care recipient means:

- Offering her the same esteem and care with which you would want to be treated if the role were reversed and you were the care recipient. Remember the Golden Rule: "In everything, do to others what you would have them do to you" (Matthew 7:12);

- Reaching out to her with sacrificial compassion[2] as Jesus teaches in his parable of the good Samaritan (Luke 10:29–37). You are like the good Samaritan in doing for your care recipient as Bible scholars state the good Samaritan did for his neighbor. "The Samaritan does . . . what the moment demands, taking care for the immediate future, no more and no less. . . . The Samaritan is the one who does what has to be done, and what he can do. This is what gives to the story its inescapable urgency."[3] As you model the good Samaritan's care, allow the love and compassion in your heart to touch your care recipient's heart.

- Placing a spiritual focus upon daily caregiving tasks. For example, when your care recipient can no longer bathe himself and you begin to assist him, approach the task with the perspective that his body is God's temple (1 Corinthians 3:16). And when your care recipient becomes forgetful and it becomes necessary to remind him of what to do and when to do it, remember that his value is based upon his God-given worth rather than upon his memory (Galatians 3:26).

- Expressing kindness. For example, when speaking with your care recipient, constantly assure her of your love. Speak kindly to her. Frequently say, "I love you." Use positive words. Affirm her, build her up, and praise her. Remind her of her strengths, talents, and skills. Compliment her. Do not always correct her or put her down; this only creates tension, irritability, and depression. Bring out her best qualities. Treat her as a special person, not as a case, patient, project, or burden.

- Empowering him. Include him in decision making. Consult with him rather than arbitrarily making decisions for him.

Ask for his help in areas of his capabilities. Everyone needs to be needed. Encourage him to share his strengths, talents, and skills with you. For example, invite him to help with kitchen and household chores and repairs, computer work, and informal child care for grandchildren as he is able. Ask him to share words of wisdom and family stories with you and others in the family. Allow him to do every personal care task of which he is capable, even if it takes him longer to accomplish than it would take you. Help him to maintain as much of his independence as possible; it is vital for his self-esteem.

- Combining past positive memories with your loved one's present situation. She was beautiful. She still is, even if she is less vital than in past years. She was your hero. She still positively influences you. She was the love of your life. You still love her dearly. She was your role model—and in your eyes she knew everything, could do everything, and helped you with everything. Now invite her to advise you about what is helpful and enjoyable for her as a care recipient. Just as your loved one's limitations do not diminish God's love for her, neither should they diminish your love for her.

- Sharing physical tenderness, if appropriate. Before you physically touch your loved one, ask for permission, especially if she previously was not one to be physically demonstrative. Offer her a tender hug; not too strong, because you don't want to cause physical pain if she is fragile. If she desires, offer her a gentle hand or foot massage (see chapter 5). Always make time for tenderness and affection.

Keep in mind that loving your care recipient requires more effort when you have negative memories from past years. When possible, remind yourself that the past is behind you. Accept God's forgiveness for both of you—and view your care recipient as one of God's loved and valued children.

Remember, it is part of your spiritual calling to love your care recipient.

LOVE YOURSELF

The third part of your threefold calling is to love yourself ("Love your neighbor as *yourself*"). Loving yourself is a response to God's divine love for you.

Unfortunately, it is tempting for caregivers to be critical of themselves. This happens in many situations, including when we make inappropriate comments to our care recipient, such as, "There is no reason you can't do this" or "Why do you do that?" or "I told you that yesterday. Can't you remember?" After we make such regrettable comments, we usually feel bad, because we know we were insensitive, and we berate ourselves silently, saying, "How could I have said such a thing! I should be able to control myself better than that. She can't help it. I wish I could take back what I said." When we follow our threefold spiritual calling, comments such as these will be less frequent. We'll also be easier on ourselves when we remember that God wants us to love ourselves.

We will never be perfect caregivers. Perfection is impossible. The only person who is perfect is Jesus. But God forgives your shortcomings. Don't be harder on yourself than God is. God loves you. Love yourself.

Do not compare yourself to other caregivers. Doing so leads to feelings of inferiority. You are who you are. God has blessed you with talents and abilities to provide compassionate and competent care to your loved one. Speak well of yourself when you talk to yourself. Be as kind and loving to yourself as you would be to your best friend if that person were in your caregiving situation.

You are important. You are so valuable that God sent his Son, Jesus, into the world for you. Jesus says to you:

- "As the Father has loved me, so have I loved you. Now remain in my love" (John 15:9). Be confident of Jesus' love, and be encouraged to love yourself.

- "Blessed are the merciful, for they will be shown mercy" (Matthew 5:7). Be assured of Jesus' compassion for you, and thereby love yourself.

- "Come to me, all you who are weary and burdened, and I

will give you rest" (Matthew 11:28). Be at peace and cast your anxiety on Jesus, who loves you. You can love yourself.

Remember, it is part of your spiritual calling to love yourself.

DON'T LOSE HEART

God has entrusted you with a holy calling: to love God, to love your care recipient, and to love yourself. Of course there will be days when you feel stressed out and consumed with caregiving challenges. Yet as you place a spiritual focus upon your caregiving role, God will fill you with inspiration and peace so that you do not lose heart.

This book provides many inspirational suggestions for how to have a spiritual focus in your caregiving as well as offers a multitude of practical tips for daily life situations. As you use these suggestions and tips, remember that you are not alone. God in Christ loves, values, comforts, and uplifts you. God bears witness to his love for you as his heart continually touches your heart with compassion and peace. Therefore take heart. Be at peace. God is with you.

SCRIPTURE

"Fear not, for I have redeemed you; I have called you by name; you are mine. When you pass through the waters, I will be with you; and when you pass through the rivers, they will not sweep over you. When you walk through the fire, you will not be burned; the flames will not set you ablaze. For I am the Lord, your God, the Holy One of Israel, your Savior. . . . You are precious and honored in my sight . . . because I love you" (Isaiah 43:1–4).

PRAYER FOR A SPIRITUAL CALLING IN CAREGIVING

O God, help me view caregiving as part of my spiritual calling in life. Keep me mindful of the sacred nature of what I do. Help me to remember that as I love and honor my care recipient, I love and honor you. Fill my heart with your loving Spirit so that I do not lose heart. I pray in the name of Jesus Christ, the Prince of Peace. Amen.

Chapter Two
Becoming and Growing
As a Caregiver

Becoming a caregiver can happen gradually or suddenly. When it happens gradually, you may not realize that you have begun to provide informal care—such as taking your loved one shopping, performing household chores, running errands, cooking meals, accompanying your loved one to medical appointments or assisting with minor medical procedures. At this point, you are just trying to be helpful—that is, until one day you realize that you are performing the tasks with regularity and your loved one has become dependent upon you.

On the other hand, when you suddenly become a caregiver, due to your loved one's serious car accident, disease, unexpected surgery, stroke, heart attack, or other crisis, you may be shocked, perplexed, and nearly overwhelmed by your new role. Your caregiving responsibilities begin immediately—whether or not you are ready for them! Take heart, this book is your guide.

My role as a caregiver evolved gradually. It took a while for me to figure out that a role was developing. Even though Mom has had a curved spine (scoliosis) and its related problems since childhood, her increasing need for care began with the relatively common problem (especially in older adults) of high blood pressure. Throughout the years, we have dealt with new problems that have developed: serious dental concerns, dizziness, vision problems, panic attacks, fibromyalgia, joint problems (arthritis, tendonitis, worn-out cartilage), and allergic reactions to medications. We attend her doctor's appointments together. When she needs to convalesce, she stays with me in my home. Both of us realize that new problems may continue to occur.

As you become your loved one's caregiver, you join more than 50 million Americans over the age of eighteen[1] who share experiences similar to yours. While at times it may seem that your role is unique, keep in mind that 59 percent of the adult population provides care or expects to provide family care in the future for a loved one.[2] Take heart, you are not alone in your experience or in your feelings.

MOTIVATIONS FOR PROVIDING CARE

Caregivers have a variety of initial motives for taking on their new role. Some reasons focus upon the *care recipient's* needs, while others focus upon the *caregiver's* needs. Scan the following reasons people become caregivers. Identify those that apply to you, and add to the list from your own experience.

- I am following my threefold spiritual calling to love God, my neighbor (care recipient), and myself.

- I want to give back to a person who has cared for me.

- I can provide better, more compassionate, and less expensive care than anyone else.

- I am fulfilling my ethical and societal obligation to provide care for my loved one.

- I want to avoid future regrets after my loved one dies. I do not want to have to say: "If only . . ." or "I should have . . ."

Motives often deepen as your relationship with your loved one becomes more intimate and as the tasks that you perform increase or become more complex. When you view your role as a sacred calling, your passion for caregiving leads you to experience the rewards and blessings of caregiving.

But caregiving can be extremely draining—emotionally and physically. If your motivation fades (over time) because you do not have the time, emotional or physical energy, or necessary skills to be an effective and gentle caregiver, it may be best for both you and your loved one to hire a professional caregiver. If this is your situation, it is best to admit the fact. Such awareness is a personal strength. Keep in mind, too, that if you do hire another to care for your loved one, you will continue to be a caregiver with a spiritual calling. The only difference will be that you will provide less hands-on care. You will always be an essential person in her life, especially as you relate to her in ways that are most comfortable and meaningful for you. Your loved one still needs you—and you need your loved one.

ANTICIPATORY CAREGIVING

Whenever possible, anticipate caregiving needs and resources *before* they become necessary. It is easier to foresee what the needs may be and to plan for them when there is no crisis than to wait, and then try to assess and locate resources in the middle of a serious situation when you need to make quick decisions. As you read this book, you will anticipate needs that may develop and also learn what resources are available to meet those needs.

The Care Recipient Information Form found in appendix A will guide you in compiling basic information about your loved one as well as help you identify which resources you and your care recipient might need in the future. Complete this form as soon as possible. Honor your loved one by consulting with him regarding his preferences. If you do not ask for his opinion, he may not accept the arrangements you make. Keep in mind, however, that some care recipients choose not to engage in such discussions because they think that anticipating problems will make them come to pass.

What might the future hold for your loved one? The following delineation of needs in older adults, originally developed by Bernice Neugarten[3] (without these age categories), and later expanded by experts in the field, will help you to anticipate how your loved one might progress through the aging process. While everyone has unique needs, these broad categories are usually on target.

- Adults ages 65–74 are generally more independent and self-sufficient. They are more capable of doing their own driving, shopping, cooking, and personal hygiene. They often seek and discover meaningful ways to use their time.

- Adults ages 75–84 generally need more assistance. Their thinking, speaking, and walking will slow down. Shopping may become a chore. Cooking may become more difficult and frequently is simplified through the use of frozen entrees and/or Meals on Wheels. They may need periodic home health care assistance and help with chores, such as housecleaning, home maintenance, and yard upkeep.

- Adults ages 85 and above tend to be more fragile. They may need special care. Home health care may be imperative for keeping these older adults in their homes rather than relocating to senior care facilities.

What might the future hold for you? Being aware of stages in the caregiving experience will help you to clarify your role as it develops over time. Dr. Rhonda J. V. Montgomery, Director of the Gerontology Center at the University of Kansas, has discerned the following seven stages in the lives of caregivers.[4] Refer to these stages periodically to assess where you are on your overall caregiving journey.

Stage One: Performing Caregiving Tasks. This dependency situation gradually emerges as you begin to assist your loved one with routine activities that she previously performed without assistance.

Stage Two: Self-Definition As a Caregiver. When you recognize that you are beginning to incorporate caregiving activities into your personal identity, you have begun to identify yourself as a caregiver.

Stage Three: Performing Personal Care Tasks. When you begin to provide personal care for your loved one, such as assistance with bathing, dressing, bladder and bowel concerns, or other aspects of personal hygiene, you have entered this new stage.

Stage Four: Seeking Assistance and Formal Services. When you seek formal outside professional services to assist you in providing informal care for your loved one, you have entered stage four.

Stage Five: Consideration of Nursing Home Placement. This stage develops when you begin to think about alternatives to informal care, become unable to continue to provide care for a variety of reasons, or fail to seek home health services early enough so that they have the opportunity to play a preventive role.

Stage Six: Institutionalization. Many care recipients die without ever residing in a nursing home; thus, not all caregivers reach this stage. Even when loved ones relocate to a nursing home, the caregiving role continues, albeit with different dynamics.

Stage Seven: Termination of the Caregiving Role. Caregiving has an explicit end for one of the following three primary reasons: death of the care recipient or the caregiver, recovery of the care recipient, or termination of the caregiving role on the part of the caregiver for whatever reason.

EMPLOYMENT ISSUES AND TIPS

Many of us hold jobs as well as care for our loved ones. Nearly six in ten caregivers, or 59 percent, are employed either full time or part time[5]—and it is not unusual for employed caregivers to go in late for work, leave early, or take time off.[6] Does this describe you?

Although balancing work and caregiving is a challenge, employment provides important blessings that go beyond maintaining our careers. Through being employed, God helps us to care for and love ourselves (the third part of our spiritual calling). Work gives us time away from caregiving, provides us with social contacts (which are often missing in caregiving) and a sense of social value, and supplies us with financial resources to use in assisting our loved ones. Thus, whenever possible, strive to be both a caregiver *and* a member of the work force.

You might ask, "How is it possible to work and be a caregiver at the same time?" The answer is to communicate well with your employer. Make an appointment with your employer to discuss your work-related caregiving concerns. Anticipate what time of the day your employer may be the most calm and try to schedule your appointment for that time. Prior to your appointment, research what caregiving benefits are available from your company or through your union. If you work for a company of fifty or more employees, familiarize yourself with the Family and Medical Leave Act (see appendix F for Web site), which might give you time off work to care for your loved one.

Make a list of things you will need to discuss with your employer. Be prepared to compromise. You may want to discuss some of the following items.

- **Flex time.** Ask if the company offers the opportunity to modify your work schedule. For example, in order for you to be effective and personable on the job, perhaps your employer would allow you to begin your workday one or two hours later (and extend your workday by the same number of hours) in order to give you more time in the morning to get your loved one started for the day.

- **Making up work.** In exchange for time to take your loved one to doctor's appointments, offer to work an extra hour or two, work through lunch, work on Saturday, or do a special project to make up the time. Be careful about using vacation time for appointments, because you will need time for rest and recreation.

- **Job sharing.** Perhaps company policy allows two persons to share the responsibilities of one job. There may be another employee who is a caregiver with similar needs and would welcome this opportunity.

- **Telephone calls and Internet.** Assure your employer that you will only make personal caregiving telephone calls during your break times and that you will use your cell phone or telephone cards for long-distance calls. Also assure your employer that you will not use company computers or company time for Internet research and e-mails related to caregiving.

- **Company caregiver benefits.** If you were previously unable to obtain this information, inquire whether your employer offers an Employee Assistance Program that includes information and referral, caregiving assessment, employee counseling, and geriatric case management.

Do follow-up work after your meeting with your employer. Write down what you discussed, as well as any decisions that were made. Keep a copy for yourself and give your employer a copy. If mutual accommodations were made to your work schedule, ask if these should be shared with your co-workers.

Be a good team player at work. Be mindful of your relationship with your work colleagues. They also are your neighbors (Luke 10:27). When they become aware that you are a caregiver, they may worry about how you will handle your work responsibilities and how you will perform on the job. Assure them that you will act responsibly.

Never take a co-worker's help for granted. If a co-worker covers for you during a loved one's doctor's appointment, offer to reciprocate when he needs a favor. Also, profusely thank your co-worker, take him out to lunch, or give him a gift.

If your job requires business travel, or if you are required to attend out-of-town training sessions, either find a family member or friend to care for your loved one or pay someone to do so. Whenever humanly possible, fulfill your team responsibilities.

Strive diligently to keep your job. Even if you decline opportunities for business travel or turn down a job transfer that might lead to a promotion, employment benefits usually outweigh the disadvantages of unemployment. Remember, at some point your caregiving role will conclude (even if it is years from now), and being employed will partly fill your void, as well as provide you with income, insurance and retirement benefits, self-esteem, and identity.

TAKE HEART

As your caregiving role evolves, daily remind yourself of your threefold spiritual calling to love God, your care recipient, and yourself. Be intentional about remembering your calling. Because of the overwhelming and often confusing nature of caregiving, it can be tempting to want to just get through the necessary tasks; however, when you place a spiritual focus on those tasks, on your loved one, and on yourself, your caregiving takes on a deeper and more rewarding dimension—the dimension of knowing God loves and guides you. Take heart and be at peace.

SCRIPTURE

"My God will meet all your needs according to his glorious riches in Christ Jesus" (Philippians 4:19).

PRAYER FOR CAREGIVERS

O God, you have called me to a sacred role that often changes each day. Please give me faith to know that you are guiding, uplifting, and strengthening me through both the challenges and the rewards of caregiving. Through your Spirit, help me to place a spiritual focus upon all that I do and all that I am. Help me also to balance employment and caregiving. In the midst of my anxieties, support me through your Son, Jesus Christ. Amen.

Chapter Three
Spiritual Nurture for Caregivers

The greatest challenge Mom and I have is dealing with her fibromyalgia. No cure or proven treatment exists for fibromyalgia. When Mom experiences physical pain (that moves to a variety of locations in her body within the course of a day or even one hour), I feel helpless because I can't fix it. When "fibro fog" compromises her ability to think at a normal rate of speed, I try and try—and pray and pray—to be patient and compassionate and give her extra time to think and speak. This is not always easy for a type-A person like me.

Viewing my caregiving role with Mom as a spiritual calling reminds me of the bigger picture of what I am about and helps me to keep going. I know that helping Mom is what God wants me to do. It is, therefore, also what I want to do. Repeating silently to myself throughout the day (and some nights) the words *caregiving is a spiritual calling* reminds me of the sacred nature of what I am about as a Christian daughter to her aging mother. My calling fills me with peace because I know that as I love and care for Mom, I also love God. Regularly remind yourself of your calling.

The exercises found in this chapter help us to live out the third part of our threefold calling: to love ourselves. These exercises help us to listen to God, to draw closer to God, and to be nurtured by God. In the process, God fills us with inner peace—and inner peace is something we caregivers need.

Thinking that we are too busy to draw close to God is one of the most destructive perspectives we can have on our caregiving journey. Make time. Find prime time, not leftover time. God wants us to stop, look, and listen—to him—in our caregiving. Even God rested on the seventh day.

You are important to God, your care recipient, and yourself. Allow God to be *your* spiritual caregiver. God will take care of you, even if you run out of energy to take care of yourself. God will fill your heart with his love, guidance, and peace.

SOLITUDE

Basic to spiritual nurture is solitude. Find a place of solitude where you can be alone with God. You may want to create a prayer corner in your home where you place a comfortable chair and a small side table. Besides your Bible and a devotional guide, you may wish to have a candle and/or some treasured spiritual reminder on your table. Make this prayer corner your "holy of holies"—that is to say, your place (at home) to draw near and listen to God. Just as Jesus frequently withdrew to a quiet place to pray, make this your quiet place with God. Prior to entering your prayer corner, turn off the television, radio, computer, and telephone ringer.

If you are an in-home caregiver, retreat to your prayer corner before your loved one awakens for the day, when she is napping, when a home health care worker is bathing her, or when she is sleeping in the evening. You will figure out the times that work best for you. Be assured, God will speak to you and fill you with peace during these times. And God's peace will carry over into the remainder of your day and night.

YOUR SPIRITUAL NURTURE APPROACH

This chapter provides a variety of ways through which you can be open to God's care. Choose the spiritual exercises that are most meaningful for you. You may decide that one exercise works best and engage in that form almost exclusively, or you may enjoy using a variety of spiritual exercises—engaging in a different exercise each day or on special days. Spiritual blessings abound in your caregiving life as you open your heart to God's heart.

AFFIRMATIONS

Affirmations are short statements that emphasize how important you are to God. Affirmations also build your self-esteem—something with which caregivers frequently need help. Peruse the following list of affirmations and/or write your own. Use only one affirmation at a time. Upon arising in the morning, look at yourself in the bathroom mirror and repeat (out loud) the affirmation several times. Do the same when you get ready for bed at night. Make the affirmation your own, so that its message automatically surfaces in your heart, mind, and spirit throughout your twenty-four-hour caregiving day. As you do so, you are allowing yourself to experience divine encouragement.

Use affirmations in a variety of locations. Repeat them when you are driving your car or running errands, when you are sitting in the doctor's office waiting room with your loved one, and when you wait in line for prescriptions at the pharmacy. Also use them when you engage in indoor or outdoor exercise, cook dinner, clean the house, and retreat to your prayer corner.

The following list provides enough affirmations to use a different one each day of the month. You could also use a different affirmation each week. Or choose an affirmation that resonates with you and use it for as long as you like. While these affirmations are not direct quotations from the Bible, they are based upon Scripture, with the biblical reference indicated in parentheses. You can also write your own affirmations.

Day 1:   I am a valuable, beautiful, and good person because I was created in God's image (Genesis 1:27, 31).

Day 2:   God wants me to have an abundant life, even as a caregiver (John 10:10).

Day 3:   God has blessed me with a variety of gifts and talents (1 Corinthians 12:4).

Day 4:   Because God loves me so much through Jesus Christ, I am called to share that love (with my care recipient) (1 John 4:11).

Day 5:   Jesus is the way, the truth, and the life (John 14:6).

Day 6:   God leads me beside still waters and restores my soul (Psalm 23:2–3).

Day 7:   God wants me to be joyful and hopeful (Romans 15:13).

Day 8:   God smiles upon me and blesses me (Numbers 6:24–26).

Day 9:   God will never fail me or leave me (Deuteronomy 31:8).

Day 10: God is the top priority in my life (Matthew 6:33).

Day 11: God takes care of me, even when I run out of energy (Isaiah 40:28–31).

Day 12: When I am afraid, I will trust in God (Psalm 56:3).

Day 13: As I pray, I am filled with the peace of Jesus Christ (Philippians 4:6–7).

Day 14: Because Jesus died for my sins, I am forgiven for my caregiving shortcomings (1 John 4:10).

Day 15: My help comes from God, who made heaven and earth (Psalm 121:1–2).

Day 16: God creates in me a clean heart and a right spirit for caregiving (Psalm 51:10).

Day 17: I am secure because God is for me and wants good things for me (Psalm 56:9).

Day 18: Through Jesus Christ, God gives me a hope-filled future (Jeremiah 29:11–13).

Day 19: All things are possible because God is with me (Matthew 19:26).

Day 20: I belong to Jesus (1 Corinthians 3:23).

Day 21: God takes care of all my needs because he loves me (Philippians 4:19).

Day 22: I am precious to God, to my loved one, and to myself (Isaiah 43:1–4).

Day 23: God has compassion upon me and understands everything I experience as a caregiver (Isaiah 54:10).

Day 24: God's good pleasure is to give me the kingdom of heaven (Luke 12:32).

Day 25: I lift up my soul to God who is always near me (Psalm 25:1–2 and James 4:8).

Day 26: God lovingly searches my heart and even turns my sighs into prayers (Romans 8:26).

Day 27: God is my strength and my deliverer (Psalm 18:1–2).

Day 28:   I am happy because God is my refuge (Psalm 34:8).

Day 29:   I am one of God's loved children (1 John 3:1).

Day 30:   God wants me to take care of myself (1 Corinthians 3:16–17).

Day 31:   God is with me 24/7 and into eternity (Matthew 28:16–20).

COUNT YOUR BLESSINGS

When we are weary with the challenges of caregiving, it is easy to lament about what we are going through. During such times it is easy to lose track of the rewarding nature of our spiritual calling. This is the very time, however, to focus upon our blessings—yes, the blessings of caregiving. They are abundant, if only we look for them.

Teach yourself to identify your caregiving blessings by writing them down—at least three—at the end of each week. These can include three things you did well. Remember, God blesses you each day—even on the most stressful days. As you list and count your blessings, you will be amazed at the number of ways in which God blesses you.

See if the following blessings from my caregiving situation apply to your experience. Modify this list and make it your own.

- It is a blessing to know that years from now I will look back upon this caregiving experience as the most important time in my life.

- It is a blessing to look into the eyes of my loved one, see the color of her eyes, the feelings in her heart, the depths of her soul.

- It is a blessing to treasure the time I still have with my care recipient, to say, "I love you" more frequently, and to get to know her on a closer personal basis before she dies.

- It is a blessing to discern the spiritual legacy that my loved one is leaving me, as I converse with her using questions from the Spiritual Journey Exercise for Individuals.[1] (See appendix D.)

- It is a blessing to view my loved one's need for assistance as a tender journey for both of us, especially as I help her to bathe, use the toilet, dress, eat, think, make decisions, and pray.

• It is a blessing to see my loved one smile at me. It is also a blessing to keep a list of times and experiences that make her smile, so that when she is discouraged I have ideas for how to bring pleasure to her life.

• It is a blessing to learn how to (or how not to) deal with suffering, seeing my care recipient as a positive (or negative) role model.

• It is a blessing to develop a greater ability to compromise, keeping in mind that it may be my loved one who makes the greatest compromises.

• It is a blessing to appreciate how valuable other people are—people such as helpful relatives and neighbors, home health care workers, care facility workers, and even strangers who offer a tender word or lend a helping hand.

LET GO AND LET GOD

Among the most difficult challenges for caregivers to admit is an inability to control the dynamics of the experience. Caregiving can be chaotic. The only person you can control is yourself, and frequently this is difficult. If you are like me, you are also like the apostle Paul, who wrote, "I do not understand what I do. For what I want to do I do not do, but what I hate I do" (Romans 7:15).

Little in the caregiving experience is in our control. We have no control over physicians who take vacations when we need them the most, home health workers who are unavailable when we have a family emergency or become sick ourselves, social service agencies that do not return our telephone calls, and fees charged by health care providers. We have no control over our loved one's forgetfulness or need for help when we are exhausted or when we have scheduled a vacation.

Taking care of ourselves includes knowing that God understands us, does not want us to be stressed out or fearful, and promises to always be present for us. God wants us to let go of our need to be in control and surrender our concerns to the One who divinely loves us. God is in control. God is our refuge and strength and our source of comfort and peace. Trust him—because he loves you. And when you find it difficult to do so, pray the Serenity Prayer: *God, grant me the serenity to accept the things I cannot change, the courage to change the things I can, and the wisdom to know the difference. Amen.*

PRAYER

Basic to all prayer is this: God is more willing to listen and respond to our prayers than we are sometimes willing or able to pray. God welcomes our prayers. Don't worry that you might pray in the wrong way. God hears all your prayers and lovingly responds to you.

God is present at all times and in all locations when you pray—whether you are sitting in your prayer corner at home, assisting your loved one with a bath, walking outdoors for exercise, driving your car, standing in line at the supermarket, or lying in bed. There is no place that God is not present.

Prayers can take a variety of forms based upon the changing caregiving dynamics in our lives. There are many ways to pray. In fact, there are as many ways to pray as there are people in the world.

Begin your prayer time (when possible) with a few minutes of solitude to help you disengage from your stress and open your heart to listen to God (as described earlier in this chapter). Fundamental to prayer is this: God's heart always touches your heart so that you do not get discouraged in your caregiving.

Here are some suggestions for how to pray.

Pray spontaneous prayers. These are prayers of praise, thanksgiving, lament, anger, intercession, or adoration. Prayers do not have to be long or flowery or well-structured. They just need to come from your heart. Pray for others and for yourself. The Bible makes it clear that Jesus invites us to pray for ourselves.

Pray prayers that other people have written. Pray the prayers included at the end of each chapter in this book. You also may want to purchase a book of prayers.

Pray memorized prayers. The Lord's Prayer is always meaningful: "Our Father which art in heaven, hallowed be thy name. Thy kingdom come. Thy will be done in earth, as it is in heaven. Give us this day our daily bread. And forgive us our debts, as we forgive our debtors. And lead us not into temptation, but deliver us from evil: For thine is the kingdom, and the power, and the glory, for ever. Amen" (Matthew 6:9–13 KJV).

Pray to simply "be" in the presence of God. Say, "O God, let me just sit and 'be' in your presence." After you pray these words, sit still and enjoy being in the quiet company of God. Just as people who are in close relationships do not always have to talk, the same is true of God and you. Enjoy being with God in quietness. When distractions occur, allow them to pass through your mind without giving your attention to them, and bring yourself back into God's presence. Feel the peace of God fill your heart as you are alone with him. If you have difficulty sleeping, this may be an effective and peaceful way for you to fall asleep.

Pray with feelings and in the Holy Spirit. All feelings are acceptable to God. God can handle your feelings better than you can—because God is bigger than your feelings. This includes feelings of anger, depression, confusion, love, joy, and any others you may experience. The apostle Paul wrote in Romans 8:26–27: "The Spirit helps us in our weakness. We do not know what we ought to pray for, but the Spirit himself intercedes for us with groans that words cannot express. And he who searches our hearts knows the mind of the Spirit, because the Spirit intercedes for the saints in accordance with God's will." Yes, take comfort when you are unable to put your feelings into words, because the Holy Spirit turns even your sighs and tears into prayer before God.

Pray by quietly meditating upon one word. Use single words, such as: *Jesus, love, hope, peace,* or other words that are important to your faith life. Spend quiet time alone with God and that word. Focus upon what the word means to you. Slowly repeat the word (either silently or aloud) over and over again. Allow God's presence to touch your heart through your meditation upon the word. If your mind wanders away from your word, restart your meditation on the same word—even if you have to do so repeatedly.

Pray throughout your caregiving actions. For example, tenderly holding your loved one's hand can be a prayer. Looking into your loved one's eyes and sharing all the love you can express through your eyes is prayer. Sharing tender conversation during mealtime with your loved one is a form of prayer. Allow your tasks of daily life to become (spoken or unspoken) prayers of love.

Pray contemplatively as you read Scripture. Mentally focus upon one person or thought in a Bible story. For example, imagine yourself to be Ruth, in the Old Testament book of Ruth, as she cares for her mother-in-law. Or allow yourself to be both Mary and Martha in the New Testament story (Luke 10:38–42), as they meet Jesus in their own ways—whether in busyness and preparation or in quiet contemplation. After you imagine that you are that individual or experience, apply the passage to your caregiving situation.

Create your own foundational prayer. Use a foundational prayer to refocus your attention upon God when your attention becomes consumed by tasks, appointments, or medical concerns. The following foundational prayers may be meaningful: "Jesus loves me, this I know, for the Bible tells me so"; "O Jesus, never allow me to be distracted from your love"; "O God, help me to see your face in the face of my loved one for whom I provide care." Close your eyes and slowly pray your foundational prayer. Reflect upon its meaning for you as you repeat the prayer. Use this prayer to bring yourself back into your threefold spiritual calling when your day becomes chaotic. A meaningful Bible passage, an affirmation, or a sentence prayer that you write can also be a helpful foundational prayer.

Pray by journaling. You do not have to be an accomplished writer to journal in a simple notebook, prayer journal, or on your computer. There are no right or wrong ways to journal. It is unnecessary to write complete sentences and well-defined paragraphs. You may just want to jot down phrases or ideas. Do not worry about grammar and punctuation. Journaling takes on the personality of the one who writes. Write about your thoughts and feelings. Share your heart, concerns, and needs with God. Perhaps you will want to draw pictures. At the end of your journal entry, write down any new areas of spiritual awareness that you discerned during this prayer time. Periodically refer back to these areas for inspiration. You can also write a letter to Jesus in which you share your heart with him; then during another prayer time, write his return letter to you. Remember that your journal is private. No one should read your journal unless you invite them to do so.

Pray with your imagination. Close your eyes and imagine Jesus sitting next to you and lovingly smiling at you. Listen to Jesus tell you that he cares for you and shares his strength, comfort, and peace with you. Enjoy being with Jesus during this prayer time.

Pray with music. Music is a gift of God that expresses the soul of the composer, performer, and listener. Open your soul to God through music and allow God to touch your heart with peace and hope.

As you pray in a variety of ways, you are reminded that God loves and cares for you—and you experience deeper meaning and peace in life. Prayer helps you focus upon your threefold spiritual calling to love God, your neighbor (care recipient), and yourself. God hears and responds to your prayers. Jesus promised, "Ask and it will be given to you; seek and you will find; knock and the door will be opened to you" (Matthew 7:7).

Remember to share prayer with your loved one.

WORSHIP

Spiritual nurture includes worshiping with other persons in a community of faith. Attend the church of your choice. If you do not have a church home, visit a number of congregations until you find one that is a good fit for you. Do not neglect this vital area of spiritual nurture, even if you need to find someone to stay with your loved one when you worship.

Why attend worship services? It is encouraging to become part of a community of people who need God. During worship you thank God for his blessings, confess your sins and are assured of God's forgiveness, hear the proclaimed and expounded Word of God, sing songs of praise, offer your gifts, and join with other worshipers in prayer. During worship your heart is touched by God's loving heart and you are encouraged.

Worship is a form of spiritual care that you and your loved one can share. If your loved one is unable to attend worship services in church, obtain video- or audiotapes of his congregation's worship services, watch religious services on television, or listen to radio services.

MEDITATION

The following meditation is designed to help you experience the love and peace of God in the midst of your complex life as a caregiver. Before you engage in this meditation, select a quiet place away from distractions—this place may be your prayer corner, a church sanctuary, or a setting in nature. Give yourself time to mentally disengage from your caregiving experience. Listening to soft, slow music may help you relax.

The more frequently you engage in this exercise, the more effectively it will encourage you in your caregiving. Keep in mind that you do not always have to use the entire exercise. Specific parts of this meditation may be more meaningful to you than others—especially at different times of the day and in certain situations. Adapt the meditation in ways that address your unique caregiving experience.

When you use this meditation upon arising in the morning, it sets the tone for your caregiving day. When you use it during the daytime, allow five minutes after you conclude to gradually transition your thoughts and feelings back into the day. When you use it at bedtime, it may be difficult to complete the exercise because you fall asleep; don't worry about that—what a peaceful way to go to sleep! Let's begin.

Meditation

Relaxing in God's love. Make yourself comfortable. Pay no attention to distractions that may be around you. Slowly relax and let the tensions in your body fall away like raindrops falling in a gentle summer rain or like ice cream gradually melting on a beautiful, warm, sunny day (pause). Allow as much time as needed for your body and mind to relax (pause).

Breathe slowly and deeply from your abdomen (pause). As you inhale, breathe in God's love (pause). As you exhale, release stress from your life (pause). The psalmist wrote, "Be still, and know that I am God" (Psalm 46:10) (pause).

Being With Jesus. Picture Jesus sitting with you and gently smiling at you (pause). Jesus loves you (pause). Jesus understands you (pause). And Jesus enjoys being with you (pause). You also love Jesus and enjoy being with him (pause). Let the following words of Jesus touch your heart:

- "As the Father has loved me, so have I loved you. Now remain in my love" (John 15:9) (pause).

- "Do not worry about your life, what you will eat or drink; or about your body, what you will wear. . . . Look at the birds of the air; they do not sow or reap or store away in barns, and yet your heavenly Father feeds them. . . . Seek first his kingdom and his righteousness, and all these things will be given to you as well" (Matthew 6:25–34) (pause).

- "Peace I leave with you; my peace I give you" (John 14:27) (pause).

Others caring for you. Reflect about caregiving. What has it meant for *you* to receive care from another person? (pause). Think about a time when you needed care (pause). How did you feel about being dependent upon the care of someone else? (pause). Think about the one who cared for you (pause). What was the most special thing that person did to help you? (pause). In what additional ways did your caregiver nurture you; or, if no one was available to help you, what would have been helpful? (pause).

Caring for your loved one. Your loved one is a child of God who was created in God's image (like you) (pause). In Genesis, God proclaims your loved one to be "very good" (like you) (pause). Recall your loved one during the times in his life when he was vital and active (pause). See your loved one at his best (pause). See God blessing him with strength and peace (pause). Remember what a special person your loved one was to you at that time (pause)—how he loved you (pause), comforted you (pause), believed in you (pause), guided you (pause), and was present for you when you most needed him (pause). Recall the love, honor, and respect you had for your loved one then (pause).

Now think of your loved one as he is today, with limitations in body, mind, or spirit (pause). Again, see your loved one as God's child who was created in God's image (like you) (pause). Hear God proclaim that he continues to be very good. Remember that God's love does not diminish just because your care recipient's health has diminished (pause). God continues to reach out—whether or not your loved one is able to walk, think clearly, take care of his own bodily needs or otherwise care for himself, or be productive in the eyes of society. Your loved one's body is a temple of the Holy Spirit (1 Corinthians 6:19) (pause). God continues to reach out to him. Ask God to help you love and honor your care recipient, even in the midst of his limitations (pause).

The apostle Paul writes: "The fruit of the Spirit is love, joy, peace, patience, kindness, goodness, faithfulness, gentleness and self-control" (Galatians 5:22–23) (pause). Picture your loved one (pause). Imagine your heart filled with the fruits of the Spirit (pause). Now communicate them to your loved one, through your eyes (pause). You are the heart and eyes of Jesus for your loved one (pause). Your spiritual calling is to love your care recipient (pause).

Comforting the caregiver. There may be times when you become weary in your caregiving, worrying about the present or the future or both (pause). You may be physically exhausted and worn out (pause). You may be lonely (pause). You may be angry that other family members do not take an active or loving role in the caregiving experience (pause). You may wonder why you and/or your loved one are suffering (pause).

Take comfort in knowing that God is with you. Pray the following prayer along with the psalmist: "O Lord, you have searched me and you know me. You know when I sit and when I rise (pause); you perceive my thoughts from afar (pause). You discern my going out and my lying down; you are familiar with all my ways (pause). . . . Search me, O God, and know my heart" (Psalm 139:1–3, 23) (pause). Now add your own words to the prayer (pause).

God has heard your prayer. Listen now to what God tells you and how God addresses your needs (pause). God cares about you. God loves you. God comforts you (pause).

Again, breathe in God's love and exhale your stress as you did at the beginning of this meditation (pause). Think of a place where you like to go to relax and to be nourished in heart, mind, and spirit. Perhaps it is your prayer corner, favorite beach, mountain, an outside park during your favorite season of the year, a museum, coffee shop, or church sanctuary. Close your eyes and imagine what it is like to be there (pause). Breathe in calmness and exhale anxiety (pause).

You still may have concerns and problems when you conclude this exercise, but let God refresh and strengthen you (pause). Let God fill you with peace (pause). Listen to God's beautiful words from the Bible: "Do not fear, for I have redeemed you; I have called you by name, you are mine. . . . You are precious in my sight, and honored, and I love you" (Isaiah 43:1, 4 NRSV) (pause).

Feel God's love and peace. Be refreshed in body, mind, and spirit. Allow God's peace to shape all your experiences as a caregiver and as a person. Amen.

READ THE BIBLE

Reading Scripture regularly provides you with inspiration, encouragement, guidance, strength, comfort, and peace. At the end of each chapter—and in appendix E—in this book are recommended Bible readings for caregivers that focus upon the theme of each chapter. When reading Scripture, it is helpful to read each passage more than once. Turn some passages into sentence prayers or foundational prayers.

SCRIPTURE

Trust in God
Jesus replied, "If you have faith as small as a mustard seed, you can say to this mountain, 'Move from here to there' and it will move. Nothing will be impossible for you" (Matthew 17:20).

Prayer
Jesus said, "Ask and it will be given to you; seek and you will find; knock and the door will be opened to you. For everyone who asks receives; he

who seeks finds; and to him who knocks, the door will be opened. Which of you, if his son asks for bread, will give him a stone? Or if he asks for a fish, will give him a snake? If you, then, though you are evil, know how to give good gifts to your children, how much more will your Father in heaven give good gifts to those who ask him!" (Matthew 7:7–11).

Renewing your heart

"Create in me a pure heart, O God, and renew a steadfast spirit within me" (Psalm 51:10).

PRAYER FOR SPIRITUAL COMFORT

Create within me, O God, faith that comforts me in the midst of my daily caregiving challenges. Help me to let go of my tendency to control life around me; instead, let me surrender my life to you. I need you every hour and minute of every day. Thank you for always being with me. Affirm my God-given being so that I recognize my value to you and to my loved one. Touch my heart with your love and keep me close to you as I live out my threefold spiritual calling: to love you, to love my care recipient, and to love myself. Amen.

Chapter Four
Psychological Nurture
for Caregivers

No matter how devoted we are to our spiritual calling, caregiving exacts an emotional toll on us, just as it did on Jesus during his earthly ministry. Some days we handle our challenges well and experience the rewards of caregiving; other days we feel frustrated, angry, depressed, guilty, or fearful. Regardless of how committed we are to helping our loved ones, doing so is frequently psychologically difficult.

At times I have tried ignoring my distressful emotions. Perhaps you have also. Yet both you and I know that's impossible. Not facing our psychological pain takes an even deeper toll.

Sharing our feelings with God in prayer comforts and strengthens us. God is bigger than our feelings and therefore can handle our negative emotions better than we can. God is there for us. God does not negatively judge us for the way we feel—neither does he want us to judge ourselves harshly. Just as God accepted all the feelings (both positive and negative) of the writers of the Old Testament psalms, so God accepts our feelings. Therefore, let us love ourselves (an important part of our threefold spiritual calling) by accepting, expressing, and constructively dealing with our feelings.

FEELINGS

Here are some common troublesome feelings that caregivers deal with. See if you experience any of them.

Depression because:

- Your role has changed from that of spouse, daughter, son, or friend to that of primary caregiver (see chapter 2).

- Your previous lifestyle is a thing of the past, and you can't see a positive future.

- Your loved one's deterioration is sad and distressful.

- You cannot make everything better for your loved one—such as curing the incurable, setting right his confusion and forgetfulness, reducing his obsessiveness, filling his emptiness, and protecting him from all risks—and sometimes you run out of patience and energy with him.

- Your loved one frequently does not return your affection due to cognitive changes in his abilities or personality.

Anger because:

- Your loved one's situation has turned your life upside down so that it seems out of control. You do not have time to quietly read the newspaper, uninterruptedly watch television, sleep late in the morning, socialize, rest, or just enjoy time alone.

- Your loved one requires care, while others around you are healthy and happy. It does not seem fair.

- Your care recipient fails to realize that you are not a mind reader who automatically knows what she needs and when she needs it.

- Other family members do not help you.

- The financial cost is impossible to meet, and you are spending your savings and retirement accounts to provide care.

Loneliness when:

- You live outside the normal lives that your friends lead. Getting your loved one through the basic activities of daily living has become your goal.

- You share what life is like as a caregiver, and other people do not understand or care.

- Your care recipient is not there for you as he once was (emotionally, spiritually, and physically), and you know that you have lost a major part of your relationship with him.

- You lose connections with people and activities that you previously enjoyed.

Fear of:

- Making a serious caregiving mistake.

- Problems that may develop next in your loved one's life situation.

- Running out of physical or psychological strength over the duration of your loved one's illness or disability.

- What will happen to your care recipient if you become ill or die.

- Running out of money to take proper care of your loved one.

- Incompetent and insensitive care from nursing home or assisted-living staff, especially when you are not there (see chapter 11).

- Your loved one's death. When she looks and feels weak, you wonder if this is her last day. You may wonder if you can handle her death and your bereavement (see chapters 12 and 13).

Embarrassment when:

- Your loved one makes inappropriate statements and demands in the presence of visitors.

- Your loved one displays unacceptable behavior, such as loudness, rudeness, lack of responsiveness, swearing, and excessively critical comments toward other people in public.

- You are unable to control the above statements and behaviors.

Unappreciated when:

- Your loved one is disagreeable and uncooperative.

- Your loved one doesn't acknowledge the accommodations you make for him, such as walking at a snail's pace because he no longer walks at a normal speed, finding a public rest room before he needs one, or planning in advance so he does not have far to walk at any given time.

- You are the primary caregiver, responsible for daily care, yet your relatives who choose not to help criticize you and think they have better solutions for the problems you encounter.

- You are a long-distance caregiver who regularly travels to your loved one's home, performs chores while you are there, spends vacation time caring for him, spends substantial money on telephone calls to emotionally support him, makes telephone calls to professional caregivers and insurance companies on behalf of your loved one, and spends a significant amount of money on care (such as purchasing groceries and medications and paying for home health care), yet the geographically closest family member (who is uninvolved or only minimally involved) criticizes you for not knowing what is happening, not helping, or not doing things the way he thinks they should be done.

Guilt when you regularly ask yourself these questions:

- Am I taking proper care of my loved one? Can I meet all of her needs?

- Why do I complain? After all, I made the decision to be my loved one's caregiver.

- How can I view myself as a good caregiver when I pursue my own personal interests, even though I hired professional home health workers to care for my loved one so I could do this?

- How can I even think about putting her in a nursing home? She cared for her parents in their old age. I should be able to do the same for her.

- I am totally worn out from taking care of her, and she needs help in areas I can't handle. I no longer have the emotional or physical strength to take care of her at home. How can I put her in a nursing home when I promised that I would never do that?

POSITIVE PSYCHOLOGICAL NURTURE

God gives us ways to work through our troublesome feelings. He does not leave us in a quagmire of wondering if we are going to survive our stressful situations. God does not want us to lose heart. Learn how to allow God to care for you psychologically.

Relate lovingly to yourself.

- Look within and listen to your heart. Know that you are a good-hearted person. Remember that what you are doing is important—to God, yourself, and your loved one. Be proud of yourself—because you are making a positive difference in your loved one's life. Give yourself a soft teddy bear hug.

- Be as patient and loving with yourself as God is with you.

- Find joy in each day, even if it is a small task that you accomplish for the first time, a new and better way of doing something, a smile on your loved one's face, or a personal outing. Take time to smell the roses. Relax, and experience the beauty in life. Dare to dream dreams—and pursue them.

- See yourself as a positive person. Imagine yourself dressed up in your favorite outfit, healthy, energetic, intelligent, confident, and vibrant. You are a loving and accomplished caregiver. Keep this image in your mind throughout the day.

- Nourish your sense of humor. Read a joke book or see a comedy movie. Laughter is good medicine. Laugh with your loved one. Together, look at newspaper cartoons or photographs of family occasions that were funny. Telephone an optimistic person who makes you feel good about yourself.

Let go of perfectionism.

- Since God does not expect more from you than you can achieve, do not expect more from yourself. Allow yourself to be imperfect. The only perfect person is Jesus. Forgive yourself for your shortcomings, as God forgives you. Do not call yourself a failure when you make a mistake. Just do the best you can.

- Live one day at a time and know that caregiving tasks are never finished. Some tasks always carry over to the next day. At the same time, concentrate on one thing at a time, instead of thinking about and trying to accomplish many tasks at once. Set priorities.

- You did not create your situation; so do not believe that you can fix everything about it.

- When you get into an achievement/success mode, remember that caregiving is more difficult than you can imagine. Write out a daily, weekly, and monthly caregiving schedule that also includes respite time away. Hire home health care.

Be flexible.

- Remember that there is almost always more than one way of accomplishing a goal or doing a task. You have options.

- Strive for both/and solutions, rather than either/or solutions to problems.

- Give yourself permission to modify schedules—for caregiving and for self-care.

- Find new ways of doing things to take care of yourself. For example, if you regularly had lunch with a friend in a restaurant prior to becoming a caregiver, rather than discontinuing this important form of support, invite her to your house for lunch or find someone (paid or volunteer) to sit with your loved one so that you can still go out for lunch with your friend.

- Rather than discontinuing your favorite form of exercise or your favorite hobby, shorten the time you engage in it (if necessary) so that it continues to be an important part of your life.

Learn new skills (both caregiving skills and other skills of interest to you).

- Because knowledge is a powerful coping mechanism, explore community education classes.

- Use the Internet to research diseases and other problems, as well as how to address them.

- Learn relaxation techniques. Learn how to meditate (see chapter 3).

- Learn how to say no.

Ask for help.

- Ask family members for help with specific needs, including sitting with your loved one while you run errands or rest—or ask if they can run errands for you.

- When friends say, "Let me know if I can do something," be ready with a list of things that will help you. Invite them to select something on the list to do. For example, if cooking isn't your thing, ask them to occasionally bring you and your loved one a meal. You may even offer to pay for it.

- Seek professional counseling.

- Join a community or church caregivers' support group or an Internet support group, and attend caregiving programs.

Deal with your anger.

- Instead of fuming as you sit with your loved one when a scheduled appointment is running late, use the time to engage in self-care exercises found in this book.

- When feeling angry with your loved one, leave the room for a short time, punch a pillow, throw darts at a dartboard (in another room), or count to ten before you say anything.

- When feeling angry because you no longer have time to pursue your favorite hobbies, get creative. If you enjoy photography, take pictures of your loved one in different situations and moods, and make a picture book. If you enjoy listening to music, listen to music with your loved one. If you have always wanted to start a Web site, work on it a little at a time—perhaps when your loved one is napping. If you enjoy congregational worship, but are unable to attend due to caregiving responsibilities, call the pastor and request a home visit or ask for home communion—or hire someone to sit with your loved one while you attend services.

- Imagine your favorite place of relaxation and pretend you are there. Feel your anger lessen.

- Frequently remind yourself, "This too shall pass."

Get adequate sleep.

- If nighttime challenges[1] prevent you from getting adequate sleep, take daytime naps, hire daytime or nighttime home health care, or use respite care services for weekend getaways or vacations.

- Follow a regular sleep schedule. Go to bed and get up at the same time each day. Have a bedtime ritual, such as praying, reading, or listening to relaxation tapes.

- Avoid caffeine, alcohol, tobacco, or large amounts of food at bedtime. Review your medications (prescribed and over-the-counter) to see if they cause insomnia.

- Purchase a sound therapy machine[2], use new pillows (they could be buckwheat, feather, or hypoallergenic for the head, neck, knees) and high-thread-count sheets, enjoy aromatherapy, or try an eye mask, warm milk or herbal tea at bedtime, relaxation exercises, or a soft night-light.

- If physical pain keeps you awake or awakens you during sleep, contact your physician.

RESPITE CARE

Respite care enables us to have time for ourselves while someone else is caring for our loved one. Respite care is essential. Don't be a martyr and say that it is unnecessary. Begin respite care *before* you think you need it! God wants you to take care of yourself. Having time to care for yourself is part of your spiritual calling.

Respite care makes it possible for us to be healthier and happier caregivers. It helps us to relax and rest, to enjoy positive relationships with our care recipients and other family members, to stay in touch with friends, to avoid or postpone institutionalization for our loved ones, and to continue doing things that we enjoy. Indeed, respite care makes it possible to have something to look forward to each day, week, month, and year!

Schedule respite care for a variety of lengths of time.

Short caregiving breaks. Take informal daily caregiving escapes when a home health care worker is present, when a neighbor visits with your loved one, or when a volunteer from a community organization or church visits. During this time find a quiet place where you can do something you enjoy, such as meditating, reading a novel, taking a bubble bath, exercising, watching a funny video, surfing the Internet, applying aromatherapy lotion for relaxation, taking a nap, listening to music, journaling, imagining a pleasant and relaxing place in your mind, singing or playing a musical instrument (I play the trumpet), holding and hugging your favorite stuffed animal, watching television, talking with a friend, or sitting and doing nothing.

A few hours at a time. Schedule two- to four-hour time blocks during which you care for yourself. Plan them in advance so that you can regularly enjoy favorite activities and events, such as attending Wednesday evening church functions, taking a community education class, participating in a caregivers' support group, or joining a bowling league. Schedule respite care for a few hours on Saturday or Sunday also so that you can attend weekend concerts, movies, athletic events, or church events. Also schedule respite care so that you can follow a regular schedule for your own appointments with physicians, dentists, therapists, and hair stylists. If necessary, hire a professional home health care worker (see chapter 6) to care for your loved one during these times, or contact an area nursing school and hire a student nurse. Provide a list of telephone numbers where you can be reached and directions for what to do in an emergency.

Extended respite time. This enables you to go on out-of-town business trips, on a vacation, or be at home by yourself. To make this possible, hire professional home health care workers or admit your loved one to a respite care facility. Assisted living centers and hospitals sometimes offer respite services. Write down your itinerary, the date you will return, telephone numbers where you can be reached by your loved one and the care provider, as well as directions for what to do in an emergency. Ask family members, friends, or neighbors to occasionally check on your loved one while you are gone. Periodically telephone your loved one to reassure one another that you are all right.

When you take an extended time away (or time alone at home), assure yourself that competent and compassionate people are caring for your loved one. If your loved one has an emergency prior to or during your time away, consult with medical professionals regarding the advisability of being gone. You may have waited and planned all year for your business trip or vacation—and paid for airline tickets, hotels, and concert tickets. Your vacation time also needed to be scheduled in advance with your employer and clients. If your loved one has an emergency, prayerfully make your decision about being away and bless your decision rather than second-guessing it.

After you have initially located respite services, develop a schedule so that you can regularly look forward to meaningful activities and events for yourself. Respite care helps you to persevere in your spiritual calling.

LOVE YOURSELF

Your threefold spiritual calling includes loving yourself. Psychologically, loving yourself means accepting all your feelings and finding ways to deal with them. The combination of psychological nurture, spiritual nurture (see chapter 3), and respite care helps you to be a happier, healthier, and more peace-filled caregiver. Just as God blessed Jesus' need to take time apart for quiet, rest, and prayer, so God blesses your need for rest.

SCRIPTURE

Depression and Anger
"He heals the brokenhearted and binds up their wounds" (Psalm 147:3).

Comfort
"I will refresh the weary and satisfy the faint" (Jeremiah 31:25).

Peace
"Peace I leave with you; my peace I give you. I do not give to you as the world gives. Do not let your hearts be troubled and do not be afraid" (John 14:27).

PRAYERS

Prayer When Angry and Depressed
God, I am so angry: at my loved one's situation, at the lack of compassionate professionals, at the system, and at the many ways in which I've lost my personal life because of caregiving. Accept my anger as you accepted Jesus' anger. Rather than turning my anger inward, where it festers in depression, help me to express it and try to turn it into creativity by using the abilities and talents you have given me. Don't let me get into the blaming mode. Especially, don't let me blame my loved one for my anger, because she (he) is also angry at the situation that has changed both our lives. Don't let me lose heart. In the name of my Savior, Jesus Christ, I pray. Amen.

Prayer When Lonely

I feel so alone, God. My caregiving lifestyle is very different from the lives of people around me. Even though I know there are other caregivers out there in this world, they do not know my care recipient, her (his) special needs, and my special challenges. When I attempt to share my experiences, some people pity me (which I don't need), give me a blank look, change the subject, tell me to see a psychiatrist, or suggest I quit being a caregiver. They do not understand what I experience—and they don't want to hear about it. I feel all alone. But you are with me! Thank you for promising never to leave me or forsake me. What would I do without you! Amen.

Prayer for Sleep

O God, sometimes I need you to remind me to go to bed. After my loved one falls asleep, I have the only private time in the entire day—for myself. It is tempting to stay up and do things I enjoy; yet I need sleep. As I collapse into bed, stop the ruminating thoughts in my mind so that I do not revisit the challenges of the day and dread the challenges of tomorrow. Help me to sleep secure under the shadow of your wings, trusting in your love for me. Fill me with your peace. In Jesus' name I pray. Amen.

Prayer for Renewal

O God, your Son Jesus regularly invited his disciples to go away with him to a quiet place to rest and renew themselves for more ministry. I also need time away so that I can be energized for more caregiving. Help me to grab times of stillness within the course of each day to be in your presence, where I can be renewed in heart and spirit. Help me also to make time to engage in the enjoyable activities that positively nourished me before I became a caregiver. And now bless me and keep me, make your face shine upon me and be gracious to me, look upon me with favor, and give me peace. In the name of the Father and of the Son and of the Holy Spirit. Amen.

Chapter Five
Basic Caregiving Tips

Many caregivers are not trained in home health care skills, nor do they have the time and opportunity to take nursing classes. Often, because we strive to balance employment with our personal lives, out of necessity we learn caregiving skills as we go. The basic caregiving tips in this chapter can make your life easier and less confused.

I've found that each caregiving day goes better when I follow these three spiritual tips.

- First, at the beginning of each day, I prayerfully ask God to set my heart on my spiritual calling—to love God, my care recipient, and myself. A sample morning prayer is included at the end of this chapter, as are other prayers that you can use throughout the day and evening. I find that my 24/7 caregiving day goes better when it is shaped by my caregiving calling and with prayer.

- Second, I remind myself to be thankful for everything Mom *can* do. No accomplishment is too small to celebrate. Because she is able to walk, I rejoice. Because she can get herself ready for bed, I rejoice. It is easy to forget that our loved ones are self-sufficient in some areas. We need to regularly remind ourselves of their abilities. Looking for the positives in their lives does not minimize the caregiving challenges we encounter; instead, it helps us not to get discouraged.

- Third, I strive to honor Mom's opinions, preferences, knowledge, and wisdom. Remember that just because your loved one needs more help now, she is not necessarily unable to think for herself.

As I follow these tips every day, caregiving becomes a heartwarming and rewarding experience. It is then that I am most able to identify the blessings of caregiving, as described in chapter 3.

ASSESSING YOUR LOVED ONE'S LIMITATIONS

Because caregiving responsibilities often increase gradually, recognizing and responding to new areas of limitation in our loved one's life is a challenge. When you become aware that your care recipient needs help in a new area, do not ignore the problem—no matter how emotionally painful it is for you to admit. Seek appropriate professional assistance, whether it is from a physician, clergy, home health nurse, professional organization (such as the Alzheimer's Association), or a social service agency.

The following lists of problem areas will help you to assess and determine (based upon frequency and severity) when to seek outside help. Keep in mind that extenuating circumstances and medical conditions sometimes cause temporary problems.

Cognitive problems. Your loved one:

- does not remember names or know what day of the week or what year it is;
- forgets special events, such as birthdays and holidays;
- forgets words, struggles to formulate simple and complete sentences, responds inappropriately in conversations, tells the same story a number of times, or asks the same question over and over again;
- forgets how to do things, such as how to use the telephone or how to balance the checkbook;
- regularly misplaces items (for example, puts ice cream in the dishwasher and dirty dishes in the refrigerator).

Behavioral problems. Your loved one:

- makes inappropriate demands, is overly critical of you, swears, uses foul language (more than usual), verbally abuses you and others, obstinately refuses assistance, or is unwilling to help himself;[1]

- takes clothes off at inappropriate times or exhibits sexual interest during inappropriate times and in inappropriate places;
- wanders away;
- fails to disclose needs and hides problems, either because he does not want to admit that he needs help or he is trying to protect you from further caregiving responsibilities;
- insists on driving a motor vehicle when he is an unsafe driver and a risk to himself or to other people.[2]

Emotional problems. Your loved one is:

- tearful and depressed;
- fearful of known and unknown factors;
- easily angered;[3]
- lonely and isolated and does not believe anyone understands her;
- bored, restless, or confused.[4]

Spiritual problems. Your loved one:

- lacks inner peace and has lost her meaning and purpose in life;
- is troubled by sin;
- wonders whether God is punishing her and asks, "Why me?";
- fears death;
- can no longer pray or attend worship and church activities.

Problems with activities of daily life. Your loved one:

- cannot get in and out of bed alone, make the bed in the morning and turn down the bed in the evening, dress and undress herself, or remember to put on clean clothes;

- cannot remember to wash her hands, brush her hair and teeth, bathe, wash her hair, or use the toilet;

- needs to be reminded of mealtimes, is unable to prepare food and set the table properly, eats with incorrect utensils, is easily distracted when eating, needs reminders to eat, leaves partially eaten meals on the kitchen table or in another location, fails to get the dishes clean when she washes them, or is unable to wash dishes;

- experiences physical difficulties with eating, such as problems chewing, swallowing, or choking;[5]

- mismanages medications. (Helpful tips are found later in this chapter.)

Medical problems (in addition to specific diseases and disabilities). Your loved one:

- walks with difficulty and sometimes falls;

- experiences shortness of breath, dizziness, or constant pain;

- hallucinates while awake or has nightmares while asleep;

- has problems with vision, hearing, teeth, or feet;

- experiences a growing number of simultaneous medical problems, including incontinence.

COMMUNICATING WITH YOUR LOVED ONE

As God makes known his love for *you*, God also calls you to share his love (and your love) with your care recipient, whose problems sometimes increase daily. By continuing to relate to your loved one as the important person he continues to be, you help him to remain positive as he experiences limitations in life.

How do you do this?

Respect and honor him. Make him feel needed, wanted, and valued. Even if he is having a bad day and does not have a smile on his face, pretend he is smiling. Validate and affirm him. If he looks good, tell him. Relating in these ways will help you to recall past pleasant times together. Practice compassion and patience by putting a smile on your face. Love him profusely.

Figure out the best time to have serious conversations with your loved one. Ask yourself if he has a best time of the day for engaging in important talk. If mornings are difficult, plan on holding significant discussions in the afternoon so that you will obtain a better response, in terms of behavior and level of awareness. Determine whether he is having a good day or a bad day. If it is a bad day, wait until a better day (if possible) to discuss important subjects. If you do not live in the same home, schedule a time to visit, even if he tells you it is unnecessary. Do not give him the impression that only your schedule is important. Be mindful of his favorite television programs, home health appointments, naptimes, and mealtimes. Offer him a choice of the specific time when you visit. This gives him a sense of control and deepens the bond between the two of you—because he knows that you listen to him and respect his preferences.

Always relate to your care recipient as a loved one, not as an interesting case. Speak to him as an adult. Do not patronize or treat him as a child. As you live out your spiritual calling, tell him that you love him and God loves him. Say the words "I love you." When you do so, also be sure to express unconditional warmth through your eyes and gestures. Be as polite with your care recipient as you would be with a stranger.

Be sensitive to poor vision and poor hearing. Try to ensure that he sees you coming by approaching him from the front. Get his attention by saying his name. You may need to state your name also, if he does not immediately recognize you. Sit down. Do not tower over him. Advise him in advance if you are going to touch him or move him around in his wheelchair. If he is hard of hearing, speak at a slower speed. Try not to shout. Sit near him so he can read your lips. If he does not understand something you say, rephrase your sentence using different words.

Be calm. Your care recipient needs to be treated with respect and honor. This is no time to rant and rave about something going on in your life or something negative your loved one did to you in years past that upset you. Speak slowly and tenderly. Listen to your voice. Be pleasant.

Unless you have something of great importance that must be discussed, follow your loved one's agenda, not yours. You have more opportunities for conversation with other people than he does. Focus upon him and what he wants to talk about. Use simple words and short sentences. Make good eye contact. Offer only one thought at a time or ask only one question at a time. Do not ask difficult questions.

Be patient. Do not rush a response. Give your care recipient time. He may need more time than you do to formulate thoughts, put words together, and respond. If he is short of breath, he may need to breathe in the middle of a sentence. Allow him to rest between sentences and interactions. If he cannot think of a word, gently and slowly provide the word; however, do not finish his sentence for him. Allow silence after he has articulated a sentence because he may want to say more. Do not jump right in. Realize that scattered thoughts are common. A new thought can come from a previous thought, a noise in the room, or even a movement in the room.

Accept what he says. Do not argue, shout, or always correct him. Do not say, "You should know better than that" or "You've said that a million times" or "Why can't you remember such and such?" Be kind. Try to be like Jesus. You are not a judge to determine what is right or wrong in your loved one's way of thinking. And remember that he has the right to change his ideas and perspectives just as you sometimes do.

Here are some topics of conversation that may be helpful and meaningful for you:

- Reminisce about enjoyable and significant life events, family members, and friends. Such reminiscence can help your loved one make sense of her life, remember her identity, or realize the importance of her life. Listen to her stories, even when you have heard them many times. Why is it that we will patiently listen to children repeat their stories but become impatient when older persons do the same?

- Look at familiar faith mementos, such as family pictures of a baptism, confirmation, first communion, or wedding, a cross, a Bible, or a devotional book, and talk about them together. Read the Bible and pray together. Listen to favorite hymns and other music.

- Tell your loved one how she has made a difference in your life. Talk about her abilities, strengths, and talents that have positively influenced you.

- Genuinely ask for her opinions, using the following questions: "What would you like?" "How do you feel?" "What is it like for you to need help now as compared to your helping others in the past?" "What would you like to do today, tomorrow, next week, next month, next year?"

- Consult appendix D (Spiritual Journey Exercise for Individuals) for numerous other meaningful topics of conversation.

As we strive to be loving conversationalists, there are some statements we should avoid making. These are common statements that people make to one another, but if we think them through logically and objectively, we will not want to make them in this circumstance. For example,

- "I know how you must be feeling." (No you don't.)

- "I know how difficult it must be for you." (No you don't.)

- "Let me know what I can do for you." (Instead, tell her what you can do. Be specific, so your loved one knows that you mean it.)

- "This is God's will." (You don't know that for certain.)

- "It could be worse." (Certainly it could, but the situation is bad enough now.)

- "Look on the bright side." (Your loved one may be unable or unwilling to see a bright side. The same may be true for you.)

Listen wholeheartedly to your loved one. You will be less likely to get discouraged if you listen to your loved one with all of your heart. As you talk together, see the face of Jesus in her face. Give your loved one your undivided attention. Don't half-listen and fail to hear her words. Respond from a loving heart. Remember your spiritual calling as a caregiver.

Listen for feelings. Look for nonverbal communication—how your loved one holds her body and how she makes (or does not make) eye contact, exhibits tension, fidgets, or pays (or does not pay) attention. Listen for key words that might be related to her feelings. Acknowledge her feelings by stating, "I'm guessing that you were scared or depressed. Were you? Tell me more about it. Your feelings are important." Repeat back to your loved one what she says so that she knows you are listening and understanding her. Remember, you do not have to fix your loved one's problems. Rather, honor her feelings and share her pain.

Facilitate good communication between your loved one and visitors by helping visitors know the best way to relate to her. For example, it may be helpful to encourage visitors to use short sentences or to speak directly into a specific ear because your loved one has trouble hearing with the other one, or remind them not to be surprised by tears, especially if she has had a stroke. When you and your loved one have visitors, respectfully honor her by including her in the conversation. You do not want your loved one to feel isolated when other people are present. Avoid monopolizing the conversation. Find other times and settings to meet your need for conversation with others. (See chapter 4: Psychological Nurture for Caregivers.)

It is sad when your care recipient is unable to speak. Remember, however, that he still may understand everything you say. He is still a valued person to God and to you. Consider purchasing a picture board so you can ask him to point to pictures of what he would like to communicate.[6]

WORKING WITH HEALTH PROFESSIONALS

You are probably not your loved one's sole medical caregiver. Remember that if we view ourselves as caregiving *coordinators*, we will realize that we do not have to do everything by ourselves. We have options. We can (and need to) ask for help—from God, other family members, and professional caregivers. Admitting our need for help is not a reflection on our competence or our lack thereof; rather, it indicates our willingness to look at the situation realistically. (See chapter 6 for detailed information about hiring home health professionals and see chapter 7 for tips on family conferences and coordinating caregiving with other family members.)

Even when we hire professional caregivers, we still need to be involved in our loved one's care. After all, we are the ones who love our care recipients and are living out a spiritual calling to care for them or see to their care. We also are the ones who regularly observe changes—both positive and negative—in their condition.

In our multifaceted role, it is important to document the changes we observe, the care we provide, and the care professionals provide. Our documentation is invaluable when we meet with physicians, nurses, social workers, pastors, and home health workers. If you have a computer, allow it to be your memory. If you have a laptop computer as I do, take it with you to appointments. If you have a desktop computer, print your loved one's records and take three copies to appointments: one copy for you, one copy for your care recipient, and one copy for the health care professional. If you do not have a computer, use a paper notebook or journal. These records reduce both your and your loved one's stress levels when health care professionals ask rapid-fire questions in a short period of time. Also, of course, document the names and positions of the health professionals, as well as their statements.

The Care Recipient Information Form in appendix A is your guide for *initially* compiling your loved one's records. After you complete this form, update it as changes occur. Date your entries describing your loved one's changing condition and the health care professionals' diagnoses and recommendations. Keep your entries short. Complete sentences are unnecessary. Accuracy is vital. Entries do not have to be made daily. (Record-keeping also indicates the changing nature of your caregiving journey.)

MEDICAL APPOINTMENTS

When you take your loved one to appointments, allow extra time for him to get ready, get into the car, and get into the building so that neither of you has to rush or worry about being late. Also allow time to use the rest room prior to the appointment. Always bring medication bottles and insurance cards.

HANDS-ON CARE

In all likelihood, you engage in a variety of types of hands-on care. Although you may not have been taught these skills, you figured them out on your own. When you need further proficiency in caregiving skills, contact local hospitals, medical clinics, the local Red Cross chapter, the Area Agency on Aging, or the Alzheimer's Association to inquire whether they offer courses. You can also pay a nurse to show you how to perform procedures specific to your loved one's situation. Here are basic tips I have gleaned from my experience.

Lifting your care recipient:

- Both of you should wear shoes with nonskid soles.

- Wash your hands thoroughly.

- Face your loved one and tell him what you are going to do before doing it.

- Position yourself close to your care recipient and place your feet approximately twelve inches apart or have one foot ahead of the other, while still keeping them apart. This will protect your back. Do not have your feet close together.

- Squat down and become level with your loved one.

- When you lift, pivot your feet instead of twisting your body. Use your leg muscles rather than your back muscles. Do not bend at the waist.

- Slow down. Many injuries occur because someone is in a hurry. Plan your moves before you make them.

- Do not pull your loved one's arms or shoulders. If you do, you may cause injury.

- Before doing a move, count out loud with your loved one, "One—two—three." Lift on the count of "three."

Transferring your care recipient into a wheelchair or other chair:

- Place a transfer belt around your loved one for safety.

- Lock both wheels of the wheelchair.

- Tell your loved one to take his time and get his balance prior to the transfer.

- If you are transferring him from a bed into a wheelchair, lower the bed (if it's a hospital bed) to the height of the wheelchair.

- Stand near the head of the bed and behind your loved one for balance and safety.

- Apply tips from the preceding section.

Pressure sores. There are simple tips you can follow to prevent painful pressure sores on your loved one's legs and buttocks. Prevention is important because such sores are difficult to heal. If he sits in a chair or wheelchair or lies in bed for extended periods of time, help him to change his position every two hours. Purchase foam cushions for wheelchair seats. Use foam or air mattresses for his bed. Before he sleeps, position a pillow between his knees or ankles to prevent rubbing.

Incontinence. If your loved one is incontinent, use high-absorbency pads or briefs. When they become wet, change them immediately, clean the area, and apply moisturizing lotion or oil. Disposable bed pads are also available to protect the sheets in case of accident.

Massage. Just as Jesus frequently used touch in his ministry, as you physically touch your loved one through simple massage, not only will she experience your tender touch, but the two of you will also make time for God to touch your hearts. This is especially true as you begin and end your massage time with shared prayer. Through gentle massage, you serve as God's hands of comfort and remind your loved one that she continues to be important both to God and to you, even with all her limitations.

Massage also serves the following purposes: (1) If your loved one tends toward an emotional outburst at a certain time of the day, giving her a massage immediately prior to that time may either lessen or prevent the eruption. (2) A massage will help a loved one who is becoming forgetful to remember your tender touch even when she is unable to remember your name. (3) If your care recipient's muscles are stiff, massage may comfort her. (4) If it is difficult for your loved one to relax before going to sleep, try massage.

How do you give a massage? By all means, consult with your loved one's primary care physician regarding the advisability of massage. You can purchase videos on the subject, make an appointment with a licensed masseuse and ask for a lesson, or gently proceed using the suggestions that follow.

As you begin a massage, focus your total energy, attention, and love upon your care recipient. Use minimal conversation so that she doesn't worry about trying to stay alert in order to reply to your words. You want her to relax. Be silently relational. If she enjoys music, softly play her favorite music in the background. Unless one of you is allergic, use aromatherapy (lotion, candles, or oil) to create a peaceful and relaxing experience for both of you. Occasionally throughout the massage, tenderly say to her, "I love you."

Warm your hands before you touch her. You can do this by applying lotion to your hands and quickly rubbing them together. Be especially careful if she has sore muscles or joints. Always remove your watch and rings so that they do not accidentally scratch her.

Hand massage. Sit on a chair facing your care recipient and follow these suggestions:[7]

- Apply lotion to your hands and rub them together quickly to warm them.

- Support your loved one's arm on your lap or on the armrest of a chair.

- Using your hands, gently apply lotion to her entire hand—one side at a time.

- Circularly stroke the back of one hand with your fingertips, supporting the hand in your other hand.

- Cup both your hands gently around her hand as you turn it over.

- Circularly stroke the inside of her palm with your fingertips.

- Cup one of your hands around each of her fingers, one at a time (while at the same time supporting her hand with your other hand), beginning with the thumb.

- As you cup each finger, slowly and gently pull your hand down the length of her thumb and each finger (one at a time), beginning with the thumb. If a finger is sore, only cup the finger. Repeat the gentle pulling several times. When finished, cup her hand between your two hands.

- Reapply lotion to your hands.

- Repeat with the second hand. Gently cradle both her hands between your hands as you conclude.

Foot massage. Sit on a chair facing your care recipient and follow these suggestions:[8]

- Have your care recipient sit in a comfortable chair.

- Soak his feet in warm water before the massage and gently towel dry them.

- After applying lotion to your hands, rubbing them together to warm them, and placing one of his feet on a towel on a pillow in your lap, put one of your hands on each side of his ankle and lower leg area. Massage up and down several times, from the ankle to the calf area.

- Using a circular motion with your thumbs under his heel and your fingers on each side of the heel, massage the heel area several times, followed by massaging the bottom of his foot with your other thumb as you hold the foot.

- Circularly massage the bottom of the big toe with the flat part of your thumb while holding the foot in your other hand.

- Place your hand on his ankle while holding his foot in your other hand. Gently cup your fingers around each toe (one at a time), pulling each toe toward you. Repeat several times.

- Run your thumb on the underside of his foot as your fingers run on top of the foot. Repeat several times before you massage the tip of the big toe.

- Place your fingers (from both hands) on top of his foot and your thumbs on the bottom of the foot. Massage, starting at the ankle and moving toward the toes. Repeat several times.

- Slowly run the base of your palm down the bottom of the foot (starting at his heel and moving toward the toes) a number of times.

- Conclude the massage by placing one hand on each side of his foot (thereby cupping the entire foot) and gently pulling toward the toes. Reapply lotion to your hands and massage the other foot.

MEDICATION MANAGEMENT

The proper use of medications is essential to the well-being of your care recipient. If your loved one is unable to remember her medication schedule, provide her with a printed schedule and do not criticize her for her shortcoming. Purchase an inexpensive plastic organizer for each day or week of the month, or purchase a computerized pill holder that can be programmed to make a sound each time she is scheduled to take medication. Your pharmacist can provide a blister pack of medications in which prescribed drugs are packaged according to when they are to be taken. Encourage (and when necessary assist) your loved one to follow the directions printed on her medication bottles regarding where to store the bottles and whether to take the pills with food. If she is unable to manage her medications, and you give them, make sure that she actually swallows them.

Use only one pharmacy, if possible. Always consult the pharmacist when your loved one is prescribed a new medication so that adverse drug interactions can be avoided. If your loved one uses a mail-order pharmacy for some medications, advise the local pharmacy of those as well.

CHOICES

Just as Jesus shared his love for people in a variety of ways, so we have choices in how to lovingly relate to our care recipient. As we do so, our caregiving role takes on a deeper meaning, which motivates us and helps us to be at peace.

Attitude. We have a choice about the kind of attitude we hold as caregivers. As our tasks change and become more complicated, we have the option whether to lament our situation, make the best of it, or place a spiritual focus on it. Sometimes we have all these attitudes in the course of a single day. Our caregiving attitude affects our ability to be happy. Our happiness and meaning in life can be determined by how well we remember our spiritual caregiving calling and by how frequently we engage in the spiritual self-care exercises found in chapter 2.

Decision making. Let us free ourselves from thinking there is only one perfect decision when we face challenges. After we pray about a decision, consider all the available facts, and consult with our care recipient when possible, we make the best decision we can. Then it is time to bless our decision rather than second-guess it. Yes, it is time to be at peace with it, because we made the decision to the best of our God-given ability.

Relationship-building activities. There are many meaningful and enjoyable activities that we can share with our loved one to help build a positive relationship. These include cooking or baking, eating a special meal, watching television or a DVD together, writing a letter or sending an e-mail to someone dear to both of us, listening to music, viewing family photographs, going to a spa, having manicures or pedicures, working on a craft, calling a favorite person on the telephone, reading Scripture, and praying. You will discover additional unique ways to build a positive relationship with your loved one.

Personal decisions. When our loved one develops limitations that prevent him from doing things he previously enjoyed, let us respectfully give him the opportunity to make decisions and feel some power in life. For example, if your loved one previously enjoyed being in charge of the kitchen and can no longer do so, invite him to make the grocery list for you, thereby selecting what he wants to eat. If he is unable to dine in restaurants, allow him to choose a restaurant and order take-out, so that he can enjoy his favorite entrees again. If he can no longer drive, ask him where he would like to go on a day outing. If he can no longer see to read, have him choose a book or magazine for you to read to him. If he can no longer attend concerts, ask him what CD or DVD (of a concert) he would like you to purchase, check out of the library, or rent via the Internet. (Keep in mind that as cognitive abilities decline, it may be helpful to suggest a few options from which he can choose.) If he can no longer attend church services, offer to arrange for a visit from his pastor. If he is unable to socialize outside his home, suggest that he invite a few friends over for a visit. Encouraging your care recipient to exercise these options is another way of loving and honoring him.

DON'T LOSE HEART

Caregiving is both challenging *and* heartwarming. The basic tips in this chapter should help you to fulfill your spiritual calling to love and honor your care recipient as you work with him on a daily basis. Remember that God is always present and helps you in all that you do. Let that thought encourage you in your caregiving.

SCRIPTURE

"You who live in the shelter of the Most High, who abide in the shadow of the Almighty, will say to the Lord, 'My refuge and my fortress; my God, in whom I trust.' For he will deliver you from the snare of the fowler and from the deadly pestilence; he will cover you with his pinions, and under his wings you will find refuge. . . . You will not fear the terror of the night, or the arrow that flies by day, or the pestilence that stalks in darkness. . . . For he will command his angels concerning you to guard you in all your

ways. *On their hands they will bear you up, so that you will not dash your foot against a stone. . . . Those who love me, I will deliver; I will protect those who know my name. When they call to me, I will answer them; I will be with them in trouble, I will rescue them and honor them"* (Psalm 91:1–6, 11–12, 14–15 NRSV).

PRAYERS

Prayer for Attentiveness

O God, sometimes in my caregiving I am so consumed with performing tasks, learning new skills, and following schedules that I lose track of the spiritual calling you have given me. Help me to be attentive to my relationship with you in all that I do. Guide me to always view my loved one as a valuable person whom I love, and not just as a person with problems. Never let me lose heart in the tasks of caregiving. Amen.

Prayer for Care Recipient

O Lord Jesus, you went about your earthly ministry doing good works, including healing the sick and infirmed, bringing peace to troubled souls, and giving strength to the weak. My loved one is facing many stressful and sometimes frightening changes in life. I entrust her (him) to you. Wipe away her (his) tears and fill her (his) heart with love and peace. Help her (him) to forgive me when I do things that cause her (him) to become angry or resentful. When she (he) is no longer able to come to you in devotion or prayer, seek her (him) out, bring peace to her (his) soul, and touch her (his) heart with your love. Amen.

Morning Prayer

O God, as the morning sky announces a new day, stir within me the true desire to be your loving servant this day. Awaken my heart to my spiritual calling to love you, my care recipient, and myself. Help me today to walk in the ways of Jesus. Let my words express your divine love. Let my hands provide a gentle and healing touch. Let my heart express your compassionate spirit. Let my eyes see you in the eyes of my loved one. Let my ears transform all my loved one's expressions into reminders that she (he) is your valued child. Let my arms cradle her (him) with your tenderness. Help her (him) to feel more loved and peaceful when I leave her (his) room than when I entered it. Mindful of her (his) special needs today, I pray for _____. *Mindful of my special needs this day, I pray for _____. Open my heart to you, so that I do not miss the messages you send me. Root my words and actions in your love and peace. In Jesus' name I pray. Amen.*

Mealtime Prayer

O God, Giver of all gifts, as we pause before this meal, we are grateful for all the blessings of life that you have given to us. Just as you nourish us spiritually with love and peace, strengthen our bodies now with this food. As we eat together may we be life to one other, as you are to us. Be with us during this mealtime. We thank you for your goodness and the food that is before us. In Jesus' name we pray. Amen.

Evening Prayer

O God, the sun has set below the horizon and the day has come to a close. I pause in gratitude for the blessings and opportunities of this day. As I enter into the stillness of the night, bless me and my loved one with peaceful sleep. Let your rest be upon us as the stars sparkle in the sky and the moonlight fills your universe with hope. Heal the weariness of our bodies and rid our souls of turmoil. Forgive me for my shortcomings this day. Grant to us a good night's rest. Yet if we should awaken during the night to more caregiving needs, bless each of us with enough alertness so that we may relate to each other with patience and love. Bless both of us this night as we place ourselves into your holy hands. For the quiet that surrounds us now and for the promise of your peace within, I thank you. Amen.

Chapter Six
Helpful Equipment and Professional Home Health Care

In God's goodness, he gifted some of his children with inventive minds and others with specialized talents to make life easier for our loved ones and us. Helpful inventions and professional home health workers give us more time and energy to love God and ourselves, as well as to enjoy quality time with our loved ones. As we utilize these kinds of help, it is easier to persevere in our caregiving.

USEFUL EQUIPMENT

Many caregivers are compelled (out of necessity) to discover for themselves equipment that will help in their caregiving. This has been, and continues to be, my situation. In fact, I can't think of even one physician who recommended a device to make Mom's life (and mine) easier at home! It has been very frustrating.

On my own, through attending national conventions on aging and caregiving, browsing through catalogs and quaint gift shops, and searching the Internet, I have discovered some wonderful inventions that make her life more comfortable and that relieve my mind because I have found something to help her. I will share my discoveries with you. These devices can save you time and alleviate some of your frustration. The cost of the more expensive items may be partially covered by Medicare Part B and your loved one's Medicare supplemental insurance, if they are prescribed by a physician. Ask your loved one's physician to do so. Community organizations sometimes lend these items. Also ask your loved one's physician to authorize a handicapped-parking sticker. Parking close to the entrance of buildings will help both of you tremendously.

Mobility help:

- cane (1- or 4-pronged with rubber-tipped ends) or walker (with wheels and legs, basket, seat, and hand-operated brakes)
- manual wheelchair, motorized wheelchair, or scooter

Kitchen help:

- covers for kitchen stove burners
- levered doorknobs and cabinet knobs
- Lazy Susans in cabinets, refrigerators, and on counters
- plates with dividers, drinking glass/cup with handle, large-handled silverware

Bedroom help:

- clothing and shoes with Velcro closures; button/zipper pullers
- hospital bed with handrails and, if needed, overhead trapeze track to assist in sitting up, adjusting position, and getting in and out of bed
- female/male urinal; bedside commode
- incontinence undergarments; incontinence bedding
- intercoms; monitors

Bathroom help:

- grab bars near the toilet and bathtub
- bath bench, handheld showerhead, spray attachment with extra long hose for the sink, hair-washing tray for use at the sink
- touchless water faucets with preset water temperatures
- harness to support a care recipient who stands at a sink or counter

Daily medical assistance:

- hearing aids; hearing amplifier for telephone
- large-numbered telephone, lighted-number telephone, hands-free telephone, portable telephone
- communication board
- pill cutter, pill crusher, computerized pill organizer/dispenser
- lighted magnifying glass; large-print books and magazines; audio-books; computerized video magnifiers; talking wristwatch and clock
- hot and cool body wraps (they come in different sizes for different areas of the body) that can be heated in the microwave or cooled in the freezer to relieve pain

General home help:

- flashing light attached to a doorbell or timer for hearing-impaired persons; pulsing strobe light smoke alarm
- adjustable small table on wheels that overhangs bed and chairs
- automated chairs and beds that help a care recipient to safely reach sitting and standing positions
- reacher for picking up items
- personal emergency response system with neck pendant or wristband that connects to a home monitoring system and telephones a trusted person for help
- health cell phones[1]
- caregiving robots[2]

Assess your loved one's home safety by evaluating whether you need to make any of the following accommodations:

- Build an outdoor ramp, enlarge doorways, adjust the tension cylinder/screw on doors, add automatic door openers to facilitate wheelchairs and walkers, install a home elevator or platform lift.

- Install handrails on both sides of a stairway, near your loved one's favorite chairs, and in other locations where your loved one regularly walks in the house.

- Place stools to sit on near the front door, in the bathroom, and in the kitchen.

- Eliminate throw rugs and loose tile to reduce the likelihood of falls. Eliminate floor and stairway clutter, including electrical cords that may cause tripping.

- Rearrange furniture to reduce falls and the chance of bumping into it; remove unstable furniture; only use safe furniture with firm armrests and non-slide legs; cover sharp edges of furniture with padding.

- Add lighting in reading areas and on stairways to reduce the likelihood of falls.

- Remove poisons (such as cleaning fluids and paint thinner), firearms, tools, and matches from your loved one's access.

- Relocate medications away from a loved one who will take it inadvisably; relocate sharp objects (such as knives, pill cutters) away from a loved one who will injure herself.

- Disconnect the stove if no one will be using it.

Contact your local pharmacist (who may sell some of the needed items), plumber, and carpenter to obtain and/or install many of the above items.

EMPLOYING HOME HEALTH CARE

One of the best things you can do for yourself as a caregiver is to hire a professional home health care worker or workers. Do so even before you think it is necessary. This is an essential way to love yourself, serve your loved one, and have more time for God.

Benefits. The benefits of home health care are many. For example, professional in-home caregivers help you to conserve your physical energy for enjoying outside interests and friendships, for working for pay outside the home, and for taking weekend breaks and vacations. You will be more relaxed, compassionate, and loving toward your care recipient when others help care for her. You will also enjoy your time with your loved one more—and your loved one will feel less guilty about being a burden to you. Remember, many care recipients want their family caregivers to continue doing things they enjoy.

Know what home health workers regularly do. Consider the following list of common home health care chores that paid workers do, and add other tasks with which you need help: bathing, helping with hair care, dressing and undressing, shaving, toileting, laundry, changing bedding, housecleaning, preparing meals, assisting with eating, managing feeding tubes, changing wound dressings, managing medications, picking up prescriptions, shopping for groceries, transferring and lifting your care recipient, assisting with walking in the home and outside, assisting with prescribed exercises, doing home repairs and heavy chores, being a social companion, playing Scrabble or checkers, escorting to fun places (such as restaurants, movies, hairdresser, museums), and escorting and transporting to medical appointments.

Evaluate needs. Prior to making arrangements for home health care, make a list of your home health needs. Especially include the tasks that are most stressful and tiring for you. For example, you may be uncomfortable with bathing your loved one because of the intimate nature of the task. Cleaning your loved one's home may be too exhausting for you because you also have your own house to clean. Perhaps you detest washing floors and cleaning bathrooms. You will be a happier caregiver when you hire home health workers to do the chores that you least like to do.

Prior to hiring. Before you hire home health workers, discuss the reasons for doing so with your loved one. Honor your loved one by requesting her input regarding areas with which she would like help. She may think of something you haven't. Ask for your loved one's preferences about the following areas and communicate them to home health workers: her preferred time to bathe and eat (and her favorite foods), her preferred exercise schedule and exercises, when and where she likes to go outside, her preferred place to sit in her home, what television programs she enjoys watching, and whether she wants home health workers to converse with her or whether she prefers silence.

Include your loved one in the interview process so that she feels comfortable with those whom you hire. If she resists home health care when it is imperative for both of you, enlist the help of her primary care physician, who may be willing to state that unless home health services are obtained, she will need to relocate to a care facility. If you and your care recipient do not utilize home health workers, she is likely to go without the assistance she needs.[3] Hiring home health care workers is critical to reducing unmet needs.

Finances and licensing. In advance of contacting agencies or independent home health workers, know the available financial resources. Ask your loved one's primary care physician to *prescribe* home health care so that Medicare will pay some of the costs—and make sure that the agency you hire is Medicare-certified. Also inquire whether your loved one's insurance policies (including long-term care insurance policies) provide home health coverage. Only hire agencies that are licensed by the state and accredited by national professional organizations, such as the Joint Commission on Accreditation of Healthcare Organizations or the Community Health Accreditation Program.

If your care recipient is without insurance coverage—and unless your loved one is almost without financial resources so that he qualifies for low-income health coverage through state and/or federal programs (consult your loved one's county social service agencies to inquire about qualifications)—you may need to pay for services. Also ask family members to contribute toward the cost of home health care.

Professional case management agency. A professional case management agency will coordinate your loved one's care, provide interdisciplinary home health workers, supervise their work, regularly evaluate your loved one's condition, and periodically hold care conferences with you. Make sure the agency you hire provides all the services you need now—and may need later. Avoid having to find a new agency at a future time when your loved one needs more assistance. When interviewing agencies, ask the following questions and add your own questions to the list:

- How long has the agency been in business? Is it licensed certified?

- How many persons does the agency employ? What are their qualifications? Does the agency conduct criminal background checks on their employees?

- Who supervises the workers? What training have the workers received? Are they trained in supportive listening skills?

- Are employees available twenty-four hours per day, seven days a week? Does the fee increase during evening and nighttime hours and weekends? What is the policy for holidays? Are substitute workers available when the primary care worker is on vacation or is ill? If so, will a substitute worker be familiar with your loved one's situation?

- Is one primary health care worker assigned to one client to ensure continuity of care and relationship? Can you interview (in advance) the primary health care worker to whom your loved one will be assigned?

- How do the workers respond to specific daily caregiving situations that you anticipate will occur with your loved one?

- How does the agency respond to emergency situations? When are you contacted?

- If transportation is needed, will the worker's driving record, insurance coverage, and vehicle's safety and cleanliness be checked? Can you go for a test drive with the worker? If you prefer a non-smoking driver, make this a stipulation.

- How frequently does the agency hold case review sessions with you and your loved one to evaluate and possibly modify the care plan?

- Request printed literature describing the agency's services and fees. Is there a sliding fee scale? What are the minimum and maximum hours of service? Try to find an agency that schedules less than four-hour time blocks.

- Does the agency complete Medicare, Medicaid, and insurance forms?

- Request references. Always call references and keep them talking long enough to obtain the information you need. Be sure to ask, "Would you hire or recommend this agency again?"

Use a professional case management agency if you can afford it. Its comprehensive care will give you more time and energy to love God, your care recipient, and yourself—your threefold spiritual calling.

Other home health care organizations. If you hire home health workers through hospitals, clinics, and public health agencies, you may need to coordinate both the tasks and the workers. Interdisciplinary workers can include registered nurses, licensed practical nurses, certified nursing assistants, physical therapists, speech therapists, occupational therapists, homemakers, housekeepers, and companions. This format for home health care is effective and less expensive sometimes than a professional case management agency. Many of the preceding questions can also be used when interviewing these workers.

Independent workers. Sometimes home health workers are available but not connected with a caregiving agency or organization. If you are interested in this type of worker, ask some of the same questions as listed above. Prior to hiring, do two things. First, consult your tax preparer so that you comply with laws regarding taxes and insurance. Second, do criminal background checks on each worker whom you hire (see below).

Criminal background checks. It is imperative that criminal background checks are conducted and completed for all home health workers who enter your loved one's home—and that they have passed the test. Even if you have to pay to have the background checks done, it is money well spent. You do not want to hire anyone who has a history of theft, physical or verbal abuse, sexual misconduct, or other inappropriate or illegal behavior. Do not minimize this concern. If you do, you may regret it later.

Request compassion. Just as *you* live out your threefold spiritual calling—to love God, neighbor (care recipient), and self—tell home health care workers that you expect *them* to treat your loved one with honor, dignity, respect, and compassion. Share the principles from this book with them so that they develop a comprehensive understanding of your expectations.

Tell the workers how important your loved one is to you, as well as how important the workers are to you. Inspire them to provide loving care, and compliment them when you observe them doing so. As you relate to them, role model for the workers how you would like them to relate to your *loved one*. Be kind, considerate, and complimentary.

Establish rules for workers. Share with your home health workers basic rules that are important for your loved one's comfort and happiness. These may include no smoking in the home, not using cell phones or watching television during work time, leaving the thermostat setting as it is, not inviting their friends or family members to your loved one's home, not taking naps during work time, and only eating food they bring from home for mealtimes with your loved one.

Be alert. When you have done everything possible to ensure that loving and competent workers serve your care recipient, continue to be on the alert for problems. You cannot rely on your loved one to share problems with you. In the worst-case scenario, workers may threaten your loved one so that he is afraid to tell you about negative experiences. Watch for the following signs of neglect or abuse: dehydration (exhibited through your loved one's weakness and confusion), malnutrition (exhibited again through weakness and confusion), poor personal hygiene, injuries, bruises, burns, an unrealistic desire to please the worker or you, unusual anxiety and stress, withdrawal, new phobias, unusual checking or savings account withdrawals, or a sudden closing of bank accounts.

Be assertive. Do not be timid with home health workers. Advocate for yourself and your loved one. Often no one advocates for your loved one except you, and no one advocates for you except yourself! Make sure that you and your loved one receive competent assistance and care.

⏤NDANT LIFE

Both you and your care recipient are loved and valued by God. God wants you to be happy and to have quality time together. Helpful equipment and professional home health care workers can make this a reality. Remember that Jesus said, "I came that they may have life, and have it abundantly" (John 10:10 NRSV). As you utilize new inventions and trained in-home caregivers, you and your loved one can experience greater happiness, individually and with each other.

SCRIPTURE

"I love the Lord, for he heard my voice; he heard my cry for mercy" (Psalm 116:1).

PRAYER FOR RELATING TO HEALTH CARE PROFESSIONALS

O God, my loved one and I live in the midst of limitations, sickness, confusion, and frailty. Grant us loving, compassionate, and competent health care professionals who listen to us and realize that we know the daily situation better than they do. Let them be your human vehicles of strength and healing for us. Just as Jesus advocated for God's people who were in need, give me courage to speak up for my loved one's best interests as well as mine. Thank you for helpful equipment and compassionate home health care workers. Caregiving isn't easy. I need your help. Thank you for supporting and guiding me every day. I pray in Jesus' name. Amen.

Chapter Seven
Caring for Parents

Caring for parents is both a joy and a challenge. When we care for two parents at the same time, it is even more complex. Let's remember that God helps us in our parent-care calling. It is a joy to know that both our parents—and we—were created in God's image and proclaimed to be "very good" (Genesis 1:31). It is a challenge to skillfully care for parents when the medical situation changes, sometimes even on a daily basis. As we encounter the joys and the challenges of parent care, let us remember that God guides, supports, and loves us as we provide care to the ones with whom we have our longest lasting relationship in life.

We adult children caregivers of parents are among a large (and growing) segment of the population. Consider these statistics:

- Nearly 22 million Americans look after parents or loved ones and also hold jobs.[1]

- Nearly two-thirds of Americans under age 60 think they will be responsible for elder care in the next 10 years.[2]

- Nearly half of all baby boomers ages 45–55 have aging parents and children under the age of 21.[3]

- The fastest growing segment of the United States' elderly population is people over 85 years of age, among whom 50 percent need caregiving help.[4]

We are not alone in providing care for our parents, even though we may often feel that way. These statistics indicate that many others share similar experiences. That is one reason caregiver support groups are so helpful.

PARENT CARE GOALS

Have you set goals for parent care? I have found that goals help me to remember that caregiving is a spiritual calling. They also help me to have a less frenzied approach to taking care of Mom. During my years as a caregiver, I have developed the following goals:

- I will help Mom to experience the same unconditional love, honor, and respect that I experienced from her when I was a child—and that I still receive from her.

- I will strive to make life easier for her.

- I will help Mom to experience deeper spiritual meaning and peace in life as I follow my spiritual caregiving calling to love God, neighbor (parent), and self.

As I focus upon these goals, not only do I grow closer to God and Mom but I also am a happier and more peace-filled caregiver. Goals can help make caregiving a more positive experience.

FACTORS THAT DETERMINE PARENTS' INDEPENDENCE

It is common for us to wonder how long our aging parents will be able to take care of themselves. Our parents worry about the same thing. The following questions can help adult children make periodic evaluations about their parents' ability to live independently:

- Are my parents safe in (and outside) their home or apartment (see chapter 6)?

- Are my parents vulnerable to being taken advantage of by telephone and mail solicitors, by neighbors who supposedly borrow items but never return them, and by door-to-door salespersons who want them to sign legal contracts for service?

- Do my parents have the ability to handle their own finances and pay their bills? Is bill paying too stressful for them due to lack of money, declining ability to do math, vision problems that make it difficult to see the numbers in the checkbook, or difficulty addressing the return envelope?

- Are my parents confused and forgetful? Do they have a form of dementia?

- Are my parents able to obtain and properly take their medications? Do they know how to obtain the best medical care? Do they know what to do in a medical emergency?

Keep in mind the following medical situations that could influence your parents' ability to remain independent:

- One-third of people over 65 have hearing problems, and half of those over 85 have hearing loss.[5] About one-third have eyesight problems serious enough to impede their mobility.[6]

- Arthritis affects more than half of women over 65.[7]

- Osteoporosis affects 25 million Americans. Of them, 80 percent are women, who lose height, develop dowager's humps, and break bones. Osteoporosis causes 1.5 million fractures a year, three hundred thousand of which are hip fractures.[8]

- Urinary incontinence affects one in ten people over 65.[9] Only half of those with incontinence report it to their physicians.[10]

- The prevalence of Alzheimer's disease and other forms of dementia doubles every five years after 65.[11] Nearly half of those 85 and older may have Alzheimer's.[12]

PERSONAL CHALLENGES FOR ADULT CHILDREN

We adult children frequently encounter three common personal challenges as we care for our parents.

Role reversal. Role reversal is as awkward and difficult for us as it is for our parents. No matter what our age, we still need our parents' nurture, support, wisdom, and love. Seeing our parents with less energy and ability to take care of themselves is a big adjustment for us. As we parent our parents, it takes time to emotionally adjust to the role reversal. To make it even more complex, we know that our parents live on in almost everything we do for them because as we care for them we are living out the lessons of life we learned from them.

Identification with parents' problems. Speculating whether we will experience the same medical, behavioral, and emotional problems when we get older as our parents do now is a common concern for us. If our parents suffer from specific diseases and debilitating handicaps, we may fear that one day we will suffer from them as well. (I have wondered if I'll develop the fibromyalgia that Mom suffers from.) Let's keep in mind that just because we have a similar genetic makeup doesn't mean that our aging process will precisely parallel theirs. Current and future medical advancements, as well as routine medical care, proper exercise, and nutrition all create a more positive outlook for us.

Ambivalent feelings. Ambivalent feelings are common for us. For example, at the same time that we love our parents, we also may be angry and resentful that declining medical conditions have made it necessary for us to take on our caregiving roles. And while we know our parents are becoming more forgetful and need our assistance, we wish that we weren't responsible for making sure the caregiving tasks are accomplished as well as possible. (By the way, lamenting how our lives have changed because of parent care does not mean that we love our parents less.) Let's accept our ambivalent feelings. If we doubt the appropriateness of how we feel, reading the Old Testament will help us to understand that the psalmists, who loved God, also became angry with God. Just as God accepted both the psalmists' worship and anger, God accepts our ambivalent feelings. We need to accept them as well—and not feel guilty that we experience them. They are part of our lives as adult children who care for our parents.

BE RESPECTFUL TOWARD PARENTS

Part of our caregiving calling includes being respectful toward our parents. When our parents experience new challenges in the aging process, let's reassure them that they continue to be important to us and to God. Sadly, sometimes we are the only people around them who give them this feeling. Let's remind them that we will not abandon them. We are the human presence of Jesus in their lives.

Let's talk with them about what they want and value their wishes. Ask, ask, ask. Ask your parents what they need—and want! Do not assume that you know what they need. If you do not ask, they might not even admit they need help, because they may fear that if they do, you will put them in a nursing home.

Value their opinions and decisions, and accommodate them whenever possible. Our parents are not always going to deal with life in the way we think is best for them. Most parents want to control their lives and make their own decisions as long as possible. They may disagree with (and even reject) our caregiving plan. They may terminate home health care workers whom we hire. If they make what we consider to be a bad decision, let's remember they have the right to make bad decisions (just as we do), unless their decisions harm them or someone else.

As we reach out to our parents with understanding, compassion, and love, we follow in Jesus' footsteps. Just as we need Jesus and other people to understand us and to be compassionate toward us, so do our parents. We need to remember that caring for them is a spiritual calling.

FAMILY CONFERENCES

Because parent care affects the entire family system, early in the caregiving journey schedule a family conference. A conference provides the opportunity to discuss our parents' caregiving situation with other family members. During a family conference, all of us hear the same information at the same time, clarify goals and issues, share feelings and support, and (hopefully) develop a consensus about treatment plans.

Who attends the conferences? Decide whom to invite. If your parents are capable, invite them to participate so that their thoughts and feelings are heard, honored, and considered. Of course invite your siblings—and perhaps their spouses. Your family history will determine whether you invite the spouses. In some families, only blood relatives (not spouses) make decisions; in other families, all participate. Even if you come from a dysfunctional family, it is important that all siblings are invited to the meeting. At the same time, however, not every relative will always choose to attend or participate in the conference or parent care. If you are an only child, consider holding a family conference with your parents' siblings, who not only may have good insights and ideas, but also may offer you much-needed support.

What are your existing family dynamics? Reviewing our psychological family history is crucial for successful family conferences. Past family dynamics influence how we care for parents *now*. Whether we review those dynamics by ourselves or with siblings, it is important to reflect upon the following questions:

- What are the spoken or unspoken shoulds and oughts in the family? (For example, "We should never talk about. . . ." "We always ought to wait for the other person to finish talking before we talk.")

- Do family members respect one another? Do some family members disapprove of others? Is anyone known to lie or take advantage of other family members?

- Do all family members work together to accomplish tasks or does one family member (for a variety of reasons) usually do them all? Why? Is there a primary caregiver in the family? Remember, while that person accepted the role, she also might resent it and need help from other family members.

- Do all family members have the ability and motivation to communicate well with one another? Does anyone in the family have a limited cognitive ability that may restrict what he can understand and/or do?

- Does the family remain together in a crisis or do family members form factions and go their separate ways? Why?

- Has there been physical or verbal abuse in the past that still affects behavior among family members? Does anyone in the family have a drug or alcohol problem? How can these problems be addressed so they do not adversely affect parent care? Is anyone currently engaging in physical or verbal abuse toward the care recipient? Remember, verbal abuse can leave permanent emotional scars.

- Is there one issue in the family that always causes conflict? Unless it relates to caregiving, keep that issue out of the caregiving discussions.

The answers to these questions directly influence how your family responds to the caregiving experience. Remember, God created each family member in his image—yet each person has unique experiences, abilities, interests, and talents.

How do we prepare for a conference? Prior to the conference find a convenient time and place to hold the meeting. If you need a neutral site due to family conflict, find one. If someone is unable to attend due to distance or illness, use a speakerphone so that person can participate.

Invite a professional to participate in the conference. A nurse, nursing assistant, or other health care professional who knows your parents' medical conditions will be invaluable for your discussion. Also, if necessary (based upon dynamics of family conflict), invite a neutral person—such as a social worker, pastor, or geriatric case manager—to facilitate the meeting and make sure the discussion does not get out of control. Keep the primary focus upon your parents' best interests and needs. Identify issues. Give each family member an equal opportunity to speak and be heard.

What are the conference rules? Through e-mail, regular mail, or telephone conversations, mutually develop the rules for your family conference before the meeting takes place. Everyone's compliance with the rules is critical to the success of the meeting. Consider the following suggestions:

- Use "I" messages only. Speak only for oneself, not for others or those who were not invited to attend (such as spouses).

- Set a time limit for each person's comments. Do not interrupt the one who is speaking.

- Encourage honesty and forthrightness. Do not judge other members' views and feelings.

- Respect your parents' rights, needs, and preferences. Watch for your parents' verbal and nonverbal communication during the meeting as well as their feelings of anxiety, withdrawal, or relief.

- Allow laughter to lighten the mood without laughing at another person's expense.

What is discussed during the conferences? Prepare a mutually agreed upon agenda prior to the conference. If a health care professional will not be present, delegate the task of bringing a medical report to the caregiver who has the most information. Having medical information readily available rather than trying to remember it saves time during the conference. Designate two family members to take notes during the meeting. By having two people do so, you will avoid biased note taking and interpretation as well as increase the likelihood that everything is covered.

Consider the following agenda for your family conference:

1. Begin with prayer.
2. What are your parents' current health situations, including treatment plans and appointment schedules? Ask for your parents' input. Remember, parents are the experts on their condition because only they know how they are feeling.
3. Do changes need to be made in the current caregiving plan? If so, what are they?
4. Can caregiving tasks be accomplished in your parents' home or is a different living situation needed? If your parents want to remain at home, try to honor this preference and accommodate their needs. Ask each family member what he or she can do to help. Sometimes older grandchildren also would like to help.
5. Should some caregiving tasks be carried out by professional caregiving agencies? If so, refer to chapter 6, and assign some-

one to research area agencies and report at the next family conference.

6. Are your parents approaching the time when it will be necessary to relocate to an assisted-living facility or a nursing home? Consult chapter 11 for tips in selecting a facility as well as other dynamics surrounding life in the new home situation. Assign someone to research area care facilities and report findings at the next family conference.

7. What financial resources are available? Consider the following sources: your parents' resources (including long-term care insurance), governmental programs, and family member contributions. Include the following caregiver expenses in your discussion: parking fees (if applicable), meals for family members who visit in hospitals and nursing homes, travel expenses for long-distance caregivers, long-distance telephone calls, specialized food supplements and clothing, medications and medical equipment, assistive technology and home safety devices (see chapter 6), home health care, assisted living or nursing home fees, and time off work.[13] Siblings who live farther away have greater expenses. Be fair with one another so that all siblings share equally in the overall costs of caregiving. Allowing one person to spend no money and another person to foot all the bills only leads to feelings of resentment and anger.

8. How does each person at the conference think the meeting went?

9. Who will be the family convener for future conferences? This needs to be a responsible family member who has organizational skills.

10. When will the next meeting be held?

While some families communicate well and have little or no strain, other families have a life history of conflict. Regardless of your situation, family conferences provide the opportunity to enhance your communication and focus upon the importance of your parents to everyone within the family system.

Remember that caregiving is part of your family's spiritual calling in life. Honor God, your parents, and yourselves by respecting one another. Help one another to find the deeper spiritual dimension of life. God loves you and calls you to love one another. Keep the faith in all that you *are* and in all that you *do* as a family.

UNINVOLVED SIBLINGS

Although the family conference is an effective way to communicate and coordinate, not all brothers and sisters choose to be involved in parent care. Face the facts: Some siblings are apathetic, some are more concerned about business opportunities, some are more consumed by their personal hobbies and other interests, and some are more interested in people outside the family than they are in helping family members, including their parents. Do not expect siblings who previously have been uninvolved in the lives of your parents to suddenly become active participants in their care.

It is also true that not all siblings love their parents. Some dislike their parents and have legitimate reasons for feeling this way. For example, they may have been physically or emotionally abused as a child—and sometimes continue (as adult children) to be berated by their parents, who tell them directly or indirectly that they are not good enough or never do anything right. Others may have been forced to work as teenagers and give their paychecks to their parents and now resent being asked to contribute financially for their care. Still other siblings harbor hurt feelings because their parents showed favoritism to others during their childhood and youth. Do not expect these siblings to relate on an intimate level with their parents.

Fortunately, some adult children have the motivation to get beyond past negative family dynamics and become loving and attentive caregivers. Others feel a high degree of family loyalty and responsibility—and view parent care as a Christian obligation (see chapter 2 regarding motivations of caregivers).

When sibling rivalry continues in parent care (sometimes parent care even exacerbates it), reconciliation between brothers and sisters can be difficult or even impossible. Do not rule out improved relationships, however. Reconciliation requires the honest (and often painful) sharing of past and present experiences and feelings. Time, patience, mutual respect, and intentionality are crucial to the process. While forgiveness and reconciliation may not take place immediately, small steps can occur as siblings talk on the telephone to coordinate parent care, go out for coffee or lunch, engage in enjoyable activities together, or attend worship services. Reconciliation can take place one step at a time.

When negative dynamics exist, develop a plan for addressing sibling conflict that is respectful of your parents. For example, if necessary, agree not to express harsh words in front of your parents or behind one another's backs. Schedule different days to visit parents—and don't infringe on each other's days. If arguments develop about the appropriateness of your parents' care plan or money management, ask your parents for their written permission to consult their physician, home health nurse, the director of nursing at the care facility where they live, attorney, power of attorney for finances, or banker. These professional persons will provide unbiased and accurate information about your parents' situation.

LIVING WITH YOUR PARENTS

Both blessings and challenges abound for us when we relocate our parents into our homes or move into their homes. A recent study conducted by the National Alliance for Caregiving reports that 24 percent of caregivers who take care of an elderly or disabled relative in the United States lived with the person they were caring for in 2003, up from 21 percent in 1997.[14]

God blesses intergenerational families who live together. When living under the same roof, we have daily opportunities to look into our parents' eyes and tell them how much we love them, to provide intimate care, to regularly listen to their feelings and concerns, to respond to their problematic situations and troublesome feelings, and to lovingly respond to their vulnerability. Living together offers the opportunity to value each moment of life that God gives us together. Near the end of our parents' lives, we also have the opportunity to talk with them about the spiritual meaning of death and the afterlife (see chapter 12).

Living with your parents, however, may or may not be for you—or even something that your parents want to do. When making such a decision, ask the following questions:

- Do you want to live with your parents? Do your parents want to live with you?

- What kind of relationship do you have with your parents? Do you enjoy spending time together? If you have a spouse and/or children, what is their relationship with your parents?

- Would it be feasible to have a trial period during which both of you could evaluate how the new living arrangement is working so that if insurmountable problems surface both of you can return to a previous arrangement or find a different living arrangement?

- Is your home large enough so that each of you will have private space? Make sure that each of you continues to have space for treasured items (such as furniture, pictures, personal television, etc.). This kind of space should also be ensured for the person who moves so that the new place will feel like home. Do physical modifications need to be made to your home to make it handicap accessible and safe for your loved one? Do bedrooms have individual thermostats to accommodate each person's preference? Will each of you have a private telephone line and Internet connection? Will each of you be able to fulfill your need for sleep?

- Are there any lifestyle differences that will cause problems? Will each of you respect the other person's decisions and life choices without trying to control or change one another, including dietary and entertainment preferences? Discuss your daily personal routines so that you can respect one another's time to get up in the morning, work time, bathroom time, naptime, medication schedule, mealtime, prayer time, and bedtime.

- How will this living arrangement affect your job? Will your parents feel safe if you work during the day or leave the house at times to run errands or pursue personal interests? Do your parents require constant care? Are respite care, home health care services, and public transportation services available in your community?

- What arrangements can be made so that when other family members come to visit they do not inconvenience you or try to change your or your parents' lives and schedules?

- If either you or your parents have a pet, does anyone in the family have an allergy to it? If the pet belongs to your parents, are you (at some point) willing to be the caretaker of the pet (including cleaning up the messes the pet makes)? If you have a pet, by all means do not make your parents take care of it (or allow it to trip or otherwise harm your parents, physically or psychologically).

- How will you divide monthly expenses? And which household tasks will each of you perform (if your parents are capable of helping)?

If after seriously considering the above questions, you mutually decide to live together, do everything you can to make it work. Regularly (not just at the beginning) evaluate how the arrangement is going for each of you so you can make any necessary adjustments. Encourage one another to be as independent as possible.

A NEW ROAD

Give thanks to God that your parents are alive. They may be on a new road—the road of aging—but you also are on a new road, one of role reversal and parent care. Your parent care journey takes you on the blessed road of experiencing their heart and soul. Remember to view parent care as a spiritual calling through which God shares his love and peace with you—and you share your love with your parents. Take heart, God is with you!

SCRIPTURE

"Rise in the presence of the aged, show respect for the elderly and revere your God" (Leviticus 19:32).

PRAYERS

Adult Children

O God, my role has reversed with my parents. It is as painful an adjustment for me as it is for them. As I live out my spiritual caregiving calling, help me relate to my parents with love, honor, and respect. Inspire me to be compassionate in all that I do. Gently hold me in your arms and calm my heart with your love and peace. I pray in Jesus' name. Amen.

Relating With Family Members

O God, I pray that you will bless our family with your divine love, strength, and guidance. As we care for our parents, help us to be compassionate with one another and communicate honestly. Inspire us to let go of our own biases and let you guide us into tender and sacred ways of taking care of our parents. Touch our hearts and minds with the ways of Jesus so that we can be more Christlike toward each other. In Jesus' name we pray. Amen.

Chapter Eight
Caring for Your Spouse

The uniqueness of being a spousal caregiver is that both your marriage vows and your threefold spiritual calling (see chapter 1) divinely direct you to care for your spouse who needs extra help. Yes, in all likelihood, your wedding vows included the following phrases: "in sickness and in health . . . until death do us part." Jesus said: " 'Love the Lord your God with all your heart and with all your soul and with all your strength and with all your mind'; and, 'Love your neighbor as yourself' " (Luke 10:27). Lovingly caring for your spouse (who needs extra help) is a sacred part of marriage.

On your wedding day both of you (hopefully) were healthy, energetic, and excited about your new life together. As husband and wife, you had wonderful plans, hopes, and dreams for the future. One of your plans may have included growing old together, as the poet Robert Browning wrote:

Grow old along with me!
The best is yet to be,
The last of life, for which the first was made:
Our times are in His hand
Who saith "A whole I planned,
Youth shows but half; trust God:
See all, nor be afraid!"[1]

Now your vows take on a more solemn meaning as your previously strong and healthy spouse needs help getting through the normal activities of daily life. Loving and cherishing your marriage partner on your wedding day was no doubt much easier than it is today, when you no longer have a relationship of mutual support. It is not easy for you, or for him. In fact, it saddens your heart and soul.

Remember that your threefold spiritual calling includes loving and caring for yourself as well as your spouse. Unfortunately, it is easy for spousal caregivers to neglect themselves, yet Jesus himself calls you to care for yourself: "Love your neighbor as *yourself*" (Luke 10:27). Spousal caregivers are no exception to Jesus' Great Commandment. Even though you might feel that you have to do everything you can for your spouse, remember that "for better or for worse" does not include allowing your own health to deteriorate to the point of serious medical problems—possibly even leading to debilitation or hospitalization.

Love and care for yourself by following the spiritual and psychological nurturing tips in chapters 3 and 4. As you do so, you will realize how important you are to God and how much God wants you to take care of yourself. When God takes care of you by directing you to new ways of caring for your spouse, be open to his leading. He knows what is best for both you and your spouse.

STATISTICS

Even though you may feel as if you are alone in your experience as a spousal caregiver, statistics prove otherwise. Providing care for a spouse is common in the later years of marriage, and it often has serious ramifications for the caregiver. For example:

- Spouses comprise approximately 62 percent of primary caregivers who live with their care recipients.[2]

- Spouses who provide 36 or more hours of weekly caregiving experience depression or anxiety at a rate six times higher than non-caregivers.[3]

- Spousal caregivers (ages 66–96) who experience caregiving-related stress have a 63 percent higher mortality rate than do senior adults who are not caregivers.[4]

Caregiver, do not minimize how important it is to take care of yourself and to allow God and others to take care of you.

GOALS

Initially, setting caregiving goals may seem unnecessary to you. You might think that trying to do whatever your spouse needs is just the natural development of married life together. Yet unless you set goals that encourage you to take care of yourself, you soon will be making statements such as the following ones that I hear over and over again from spousal caregivers:

"I'm always tired and fatigued."

"I shouldn't complain, but . . ."

"I have no time for myself, not even one minute."

"Sometimes I think my spouse tries to manipulate and control me. This isn't the way he was in the past."

"No one ever asks me what I need."

No matter how long you have been married or how deeply you love your spouse, you need to set caregiving goals. Consider adapting the following goals to your situation; then add other personal goals as well:

- I will remind myself every day that caring for my spouse is a spiritual calling.

- I will be open to new ways in which God may guide me in caring for my spouse.

- I will remember to take care of myself so that I do not also suffer ill health because of the strain of my caregiving responsibilities.

Goals such as these can help you over the course of time to experience caregiving more positively. As you live out these goals, your relationship with your spouse can be one in which both of you receive care, if not from one another, at least from God, yourself, and other people. Your heart and spirit will be nourished as well as your spouse's.

PERSONAL CHALLENGES OF YOUR CHANGING RELATIONSHIP

Your marital relationship changes when your spouse needs extra care. In fact, both of you will be forced to make adjustments in your life together. You need to provide more care and support. Your spouse needs to learn to receive care. Both of you also need to accept and acknowledge that you (the caregiver spouse) cannot do everything for both of you any more than your loved one can completely take care of himself. Both of you have limitations.

Here are some common challenges that affect the marital relationship when one of you needs extra care and the other becomes the care provider.

Cause of situation. In all likelihood you did not do anything to cause the situation that resulted in your spouse's need for extra help. Do not blame yourself, and do not allow anyone (such as your spouse, children, stepchildren, friends) to blame you either, even subtly. You cannot prevent physical disease or psychological illness. And if an accident led to your caregiving situation, that's just what it was: an *accident*. Do not look to yourself as the cause, and do not allow the real cause of the problem to adversely affect your relationship with your spouse. Remember, you are positively responding to your new situation by providing care for your lifelong partner.

Balancing time. Just as was true earlier in your marriage when both of you were active and vital, now that one of you is a caregiver and the other is a care recipient, one of your challenges remains that of balancing time alone and time together. It is important that each of you tells the other when you need to be alone. You might want to schedule time to be alone each day. Balance this with quality time together (apart from time when caregiving tasks need to be performed)—when your whole focus is upon the other person and your relationship. Your "together" time can also be called your "dating time." Be gentle and compassionate during this special time together. Cherish one another. Smile at each other and, if possible, do something kind for one another. Do not go to bed at night angry with each other. Creating a balance of time alone and time together nourishes and sustains your relationship.

Communication problems. If your spouse has a physical or psychological illness (such as dementia) and is unable to communicate with you as in the past, you may find it difficult to see her as the person you fell in love with years ago and the one you have lived with for many years. If her personality has changed, some of the normalcy of your marital relationship is gone. Due to her inability to communicate well, you cannot rely upon your spouse to relate to you as in the past or help you make decisions about running your household and taking care of daily responsibilities. Many decisions are up to you alone because your spouse's ability to converse effectively is compromised. See chapter 5 for tips about communication.

Spirituality. When your spouse is ill and both of you become homebound due to caregiving responsibilities, you can grow closer to God and one another, even if you are unable to attend church services in your congregation. Ask your congregation for cassette tapes or DVDs of the worship services. View the services together, participating also (as you are able) in the singing and the praying. Ask your pastor to visit in your home on a regular basis and bring Communion. Watch Christian videos together (such as *Jesus of Nazareth* or *The Visual Bible*). Occasionally ask a member of your congregation to sit with your spouse (or hire respite care) so that you can attend worship services. Engage in as many forms of spiritual care as you can (see chapter 3). Remember, loving God is part of your threefold spiritual calling.

Sex. Caregivers come to realize that the sexual intimacy they enjoyed earlier in their marriage may have changed due to their partner's illness (and medications) or handicap. If your spouse is capable of talking about this intimate problem, it is important to share your feelings and frustrations with one another. Consult your physician about the problem. There may be a treatment that can help the situation. If not, transition to tender and gentle touch. Hold hands. Hug. Snuggle and express affection and love for one another in other loving ways.

Travel limitations. Your relationship changes drastically when your spouse can no longer get into a car. When this happens, you cannot do things that you previously enjoyed together, such as going to a favorite restaurant, attending family events, going to the theater, or traveling to faraway destinations. In addition to losing your freedom, you lose the shared experience that lingers long past the actual event. Now you wonder, *Am I being selfish if I go by myself or go with others (such as with friends, family members, or a tour group)?* Ask yourself what your spouse would want you to do—and what he would do if the situation were reversed. If you occasionally choose to go places, you may wish to share pictures and details of the event with your spouse (if he enjoys hearing about your experiences).

Relocation to a warmer climate. Due to a spouse's health problems, sometimes the couple relocates to a warmer climate—whether for the winter or permanently. Be cautious about doing so. Both of you may initially be excited about the adventure of moving. After you move, however (and your spouse's condition possibly deteriorates), you might not have anyone near you to offer emotional, physical, or spiritual support. Even transporting your spouse to medical appointments may be difficult. Plus, if your spouse dies, you may have no one to help you make funeral or memorial service arrangements from afar. You also may be unable to drive home alone. If you fly home, packing your belongings by yourself and arranging for them to be transported also may be difficult and confusing. Thus while relocation initially may seem to be ideal for you as a couple, it can lead to serious problems for you, the spousal caregiver.

Care facilities. If it becomes necessary for your spouse to be admitted to a care facility, you will, of course, experience other changes in your relationship, such as the physical loss of your spouse at home, which lead to many other kinds of adjustments. Although you and your spouse may have previously promised that you would never put each other in a care facility, sometimes it is unavoidable. Read chapter 11 on how to choose a care facility and tips on visiting your loved one in a care facility.

CAN YOU CARE FOR YOUR SPOUSE AT HOME?

If prior to being a caregiver your marital relationship was happy and satisfactory, you may be better able to provide care at home. If, however, your marriage had problems before your spouse began to need extra help, know that those troubles are not going to disappear. They may worsen. If your spouse's personality changes due to his medical condition or medications, or if he needs the kind of 24/7 care that is impossible for one person to provide, it will be difficult to keep him at home.

Use your caregiving goals and the following questions to periodically evaluate your ability to care for your spouse at home. Do this at least every *three* months because it is easy for caregivers to be so involved in what they are doing that they lose their objectivity. Spousal caregivers (as statistics indicate) are prone to developing their own physical and psychological health problems as they care for their loved one. Thus, regularly evaluate how you are handling the situation and whether you need to make changes. The following questions can help you.

PSYCHOLOGICAL EVALUATION

Remember to consult chapter 4 for tips on handling your feelings. Then, on a scale of 1 to 10, with 10 being highest and most problematic, rate yourself on each question.

- **Do you feel overwhelmed with your overall spousal caregiving experience?** Perhaps caregiving has become the focus of your entire life. Out of necessity, you may have given up those areas of life that previously brought you enjoyment. You may be stressed out. You may have a difficult time concentrating, and sometimes you may even forget the ordinary things, such as turning off the stove, locking the doors at night, and neglecting other safety issues. The intensity and complexity of caring for your spouse may have become more than you can handle.

(Least overwhelmed) 1 2 3 4 5 6 7 8 9 10 (Greatly overwhelmed)

- **Do you feel resentful that you have to provide extensive care for your spouse?** Even though on your wedding day you promised to love and care for your spouse, because of the enormous care he now needs, you might no longer enjoy being with him. At times you may be repulsed by the intimate tasks that you never imagined having to do for him. You also may resent the so-called easier tasks. For example, even though your spouse's physician states that a special diet is imperative for your spouse's well-being, you resent this new way of having to cook. It is a lot of work—and, besides, you are too tired from all the other daily caregiving tasks to spend extensive time on cooking and cleanup. You also deeply resent your new role because you know that in spite of everything you are doing for him, he will never be able to help you if you need assistance later in life.

(No resentment) 1 2 3 4 5 6 7 8 9 10 (High level of resentment)

- **Do you frequently feel angry?** It doesn't seem fair. You and others expect you to be a good caregiver, yet you are not prepared to handle the situation. And no one offers to help you! Plus, your spouse takes it for granted that you will do everything for her—and she shows no appreciation for what you do. You live with constant irritation and tension. Sometimes you are so angry that you yell at your spouse, use bad language that you never used before, threaten that you'll quit taking care of her or admit her to a care facility, or even hit or shake her. Sometimes it seems as if you cannot control your anger because you cannot control the situation.

(No anger) 1 2 3 4 5 6 7 8 9 10 (High level of anger)

- **Do you frequently become depressed, cry a lot, or have feelings of hopelessness?** Because your identity may now have shifted from that of spouse to that of full-time spousal caregiver, you feel almost a constant sadness about your spouse's medical limitations as well as your limitations in being able to provide care. You have started to prefer isolation—and do not want to talk to anyone anymore—even though this leads to loneliness and deeper depression. You have lost your energy and inspiration for caring for your spouse (and yourself). Almost everything in your married life together is different—and you are sad. You frequently shed tears and feel hopeless.

(No depression) 1 2 3 4 5 6 7 8 9 10 (Deep depression)

PHYSICAL EVALUATION

Again, on a scale of 1 to 10, with 10 being highest and most problematic, rate yourself on each question.

- **Has your physical health seriously deteriorated due to the rigors of caregiving?** You may be providing as much 24/7 care at home as your spouse would receive in a care facility. Your physical tasks may include bringing water or a nutritional drink every two hours to prevent dehydration, cooking meals and feeding him, bathing him (and he may be a large and heavy person), dealing with the unpleasantness of incontinence and gastrointestinal problems, lifting and transferring him from bed to chair, obtaining and administering medications, performing medical procedures (such as dressing changes, physical therapy home exercises, changing colostomy bags), helping him walk, taking him to doctor's appointments, and other physically exhausting tasks for you. As a result, you may experience backaches, tiredness, stiffness, weakness, dizziness, and weight change. You also may be sleep-deprived because, for example, your spouse is restless during the night and keeps you awake. He also may have trouble breathing, even when on oxygen, so not only do you worry about whether he will live through the night, but his breathing is disturbingly loud also. He may cough, pace, or need assistance in the bathroom a number of times during the night. Caregiving takes an enormous physical toll on you.

(None) 1 2 3 4 5 6 7 8 9 10 (Exhaustive physical problems)

- **Have you developed serious medical problems of your own?** During your years of caregiving, you may develop common illnesses and diseases that prevent you from caring for your spouse. Some of these can include cancer, heart disease, arthritis, fibromyalgia, dementia, osteoporosis, visual impairment, a broken limb, pneumonia, and other long-term medical conditions and hospitalizations that make it impossible to be a caregiver.

(None) 1 2 3 4 5 6 7 8 9 10 (Serious medical problems)

- **Are you at the point of needing more time away from your spouse than respite care can provide?** (See chapter 6 for more information about respite care.) Even if you regularly schedule respite care, you still may be exhausted. Before you can barely move around and function as a caregiver, you need more rest.

(None) 1 2 3 4 5 6 7 8 9 10 (In great need of more time for yourself)

- **Are professional caregivers telling you that you can no longer keep your spouse at home?** If they are, listen to them. If your wife is enrolled in adult care and the staff tells you that they cannot handle her any longer, neither can you. If your caregiver support group members say, "You can't do it anymore," they are objectively concerned about you. If professional home health care workers suggest that you find a new living arrangement for your spouse, they are thinking about your well-being as well as hers. If your physician tells you that your spouse's needs are greater than what you can provide, heed the advice.

(None) 1 2 3 4 5 6 7 8 9 10 (Strong professional recommendations)

OTHER FACTORS TO EVALUATE

Again, on a scale of 1 to 10, with 10 being highest and most problematic, rate yourself on each question.

- **Has all of life become too complicated to handle by yourself?** You have already evaluated your psychological and physical ability related to being able to care for your spouse at home. You also know, however, that more is required of you than caregiving. Look at this bigger picture of your life: shopping, cooking, running errands, laundry, housecleaning, home maintenance, yard work (summer and winter), finding and supervising home health workers, transportation, finding and installing handicap-accessible equipment in your home, communicating with family members, and handling your finances and paper work (including keeping up with regular monthly bill paying, paying for medications and specialized medical supplies and equipment, paying for home modifications, and transportation costs). Sometimes life becomes too much!

(No problems) 1 2 3 4 5 6 7 8 9 10 (Can no longer handle it all)

- **Is your spouse physically, verbally, or sexually abusive?**
  Know that abuse is unacceptable, even from a spouse who is dependent upon you for care. Consult your spouse's physician if you are a victim of abuse. Occasionally a physician can prescribe a mood-altering medication that may improve a person's behavior.

What forms does abuse take? Here are some samples:

- throwing things at the caregiver
- hitting the caregiver with a fist or cane
- attacking the caregiver with a knife
- inflicting subtle abuse, such as closing his eyes, refusing to talk, and refusing to cooperate with the caregiver
- controlling the caregiver's life by not allowing her to spend time with others
- not allowing other people to visit in the home or help with caregiving tasks
- threatening to injure, rape, or kill the caregiver (the fear connected with this possibility is abusive)

When any form of abuse occurs, the marital relationship can deteriorate to the point that the caregiver looks forward to the abuser being admitted to a care facility or even dying in order to end the abuse. If your spouse is abusive or potentially abusive, seek help—and always remove all guns and other weapons from the house. You are considered a vulnerable adult when your spouse is abusive. Contact your county's Adult Protective Services to make an evaluation of your situation and find a solution. Abuse cannot be tolerated in a marital relationship, even in a caregiving situation.
(None) 1 2 3 4 5 6 7 8 9 10 (High level of abuse)

Now summarize how you have rated yourself in each category and objectively interpret your results.

Category	Level
Overwhelmed	1 2 3 4 5 6 7 8 9 10
Resentment	1 2 3 4 5 6 7 8 9 10
Anger	1 2 3 4 5 6 7 8 9 10
Depression	1 2 3 4 5 6 7 8 9 10
Physical health deterioration	1 2 3 4 5 6 7 8 9 10
Serious medical problem(s)	1 2 3 4 5 6 7 8 9 10
Need more time for self	1 2 3 4 5 6 7 8 9 10
Professional recommendations	1 2 3 4 5 6 7 8 9 10
Life's responsibilities are too much	1 2 3 4 5 6 7 8 9 10
Abuse	1 2 3 4 5 6 7 8 9 10

You may want to discuss your results with a trusted person. If so, have that person objectively help you decide whether you can continue providing care for your spouse at home or whether admission to a care facility (see chapter 11) is necessary. If the majority of your answers are on the highest end of the scale, your decision should be clear.

Remember, if you decide to continue as your spouse's caregiver, do this evaluation every three months, because your situation may change.

INVOLVING OTHER FAMILY MEMBERS

While some parents are blessed with close emotional ties to their adult children who want to help, others are not. Some parents may have adult children who are in poor health (perhaps suffering from early-onset Alzheimer's, cancer, or physical disability) and cannot help, or children who cannot financially afford to help, even when they want to do so. Not all couples have children. When there are no children or when adult children choose not to help, spousal caregivers need to figure out for themselves how to provide care. (This book is one way to do so.) Parents who have only one child need to remember that an only child carries an especially heavy burden when helping with caregiving.

If your dependent spouse has children by a previous marriage, you may receive either help or interference. Hopefully, the children will help you in caring for their parent. Some stepchildren, however, think they should be in control of caring for their parent rather than you. This can be a difficult situation.

It is up to you whether you choose to involve adult children. (If you do not, you may consider asking either your siblings or your spouse's siblings to help if they are able.) When you choose to involve family members in the caregiving experience, share your goals with them. Make sure they understand the spiritual nature of what you are doing. Ask them to place a spiritual focus upon their caregiving role so that they will find meaning in what they do as well as relate to your spouse (their parent) with love and honor. Encourage your children to read the chapters of this book that apply to them (especially chapter 7). As they learn more about caregiving, they will be better able to help you and your spouse. You may even want to give each of them their own copy of this book.

Involve your adult children as soon as possible. If you don't, they will probably figure out your situation anyway by observing the toll it takes on you. You may want to protect them by not sharing the gravity of the situation. But if you aren't honest with them, they might feel hurt and eventually ask you, "Why couldn't you put your trust in us?"

Do not be embarrassed to discuss your care recipient's situation with family members. Do not make up excuses for your spouse's behavior. Tell it like it is. Name the problem, whether it is cancer, Alzheimer's, schizophrenia, or anything else. Describe the symptoms as well. And keep your children up to date on new developments in your spouse's situation.

Advise your children how they can help you. Keep in mind that not everyone has the same ability or desire to help. You may want to ask your most responsible adult child to be *your* primary caregiver and consultant. That person can communicate with your other children (if others want to help). Be specific about what your needs might be. For example, tell your children:

- "At times I may need to request your help in getting a specific task accomplished, such as finding someone to do yard work, paper work, a hands-on task with my spouse, or hiring home health care."

- "Allow me space and control over my life, even when I ride the roller coaster of caregiving's ups and downs."

- "Sometimes I will telephone you when I need an unscheduled respite break. I do not always expect you to provide the respite care, but I might need you to help me make arrangements for it. Also [if it is true for you] the best kind of respite care for me would be to rest in my home, sleep in my own bed, and eat my own kinds of food. This might mean our loved one will need to be admitted to a respite care center for a period of time."

- "If our loved one sometime tells you that she refuses to have anyone else care for her other than me, be firm—because unless outside help is utilized, we both may wind up in a medical crisis and need to relocate to a care facility together."

- "If the time comes when I lose my objectivity about how much care I can provide for her, I want you to intervene. I give you permission to step in and insist that a change be made. This will be a relief to me. And for any protesting I might do at that point, I apologize to you now—and thank you in advance for taking charge."

- "If I become critically ill or even die, you will be responsible for taking over the caregiving responsibilities. Refer to the Care Recipient Information Form that I have been continually updating in appendix A for both of us. Also refer to our funeral or memorial service plans that we completed for ourselves. They are found in appendix B."

Whatever your circumstances, a family conference can help facilitate communication. See chapter 7 for tips on how to hold a family conference.

TAKE CARE

Being a spousal caregiver involves caring for yourself as well as your spouse. Unless you take care of yourself, you will be unable to care for her. Your threefold spiritual calling reminds you of the importance of loving yourself (and your spouse). Also remember to always make time for God, because "he cares for you" (1 Peter 5:7).

SCRIPTURE

"God is our refuge and strength, an ever-present help in trouble" (Psalm 46:1).

PRAYER

O God, it is so difficult to adjust to this new marital relationship of being a caregiver to my spouse because she (he) needs extra help. I long for the days when we enjoyed doing things together. Now we are together, but it is different: she (he) needs a lot of help from me—and I need a lot of help from you and others to care for her (him). My refuge is in you. I pray that you will continue to give me strength. I also pray for wisdom to know if and when she (he) may need more help than I can provide. Bless me with this wisdom, I pray. In Jesus' name. Amen.

Chapter Nine
Long-Distance Caregiving

We are just as important to our care recipients when we live geographically distant as are family members who live nearby. Our care recipients need us. And sometimes those of us who live an airplane flight or driving trip away are more involved in caregiving than those who live down the street from our loved ones.

As a long-distance caregiver myself, I know firsthand what it is like to be a four-hour flight away from Mom, a four-hour drive (one way), and a seventy-five-minute drive away. Long-distance caregivers also know that our actual travel time is even greater when we add the time it takes to pack for our trip, drive to the airport, find a parking space and our gate, and wait for our flight to depart—or to service our car before we travel, load our belongings into our car, and stop at gas stations for rest breaks as well as gas.

Long-distance caregivers expend enormous physical, psychological, and spiritual energy during the planning and preparation for travel, during the actual travel time, during our visit with our loved one, during our return trip, and during the reentry to our personal life (such as unpacking, doing laundry, restocking our refrigerators, and transitioning back into our employment setting, where no one has a clue what we have just experienced). Being a long-distance caregiver is exhausting.

God knows that long-distance caregivers are special people. God is the One who loves, understands, guides, and strengthens us when we are pulled in many directions. He comforts us in our lonely experience and reminds us that his only Son, Jesus, also understands what we are going through, because Jesus too was a mobile caregiver. God knows that caregiving isn't easy for us. He indeed blesses us for going the extra mile in helping our loved ones who need care.

As we live out our long-distance spiritual calling, God says: "I will instruct you and teach you in the way you should go; I will counsel you and watch over you" (Psalm 32:8). Take heart and be at peace. God, who guides you, is always with you—in the airplane, in the car, and in your loved one's place of residence.

STATISTICS

Do you ever wonder how many of us long-distance caregivers are out there in our mobile society? Although it often seems as if we are alone, currently more than five million Americans provide care from afar.[1] They experience similar challenges to ours. In the near future there will be an even higher percentage of us helping aging parents. Statistics indicate that the number of persons providing long-distance care will double in the next 15 years.[2]

Who is included in these statistics? Generally speaking, you are a long-distance caregiver if you live far enough away from your loved one's home to make it impossible to be involved in her daily activities of living. Long-distance caregivers cannot be there every day.

How long will you be a long-distance caregiver? The length of time varies. While the average age of the long-distance care recipient is 78 years,[3] ongoing medical advances (that lead to longer life spans) mean that your role as a long-distance caregiver could extend into your retirement years, unless you choose to terminate your role due to exhaustion, personal health problems, or other reasons.

PRIMARY CAREGIVER: WHO IS IT?

If you have siblings or other family members who live near your care recipient, figuring out who the primary caregiver is may not be easy. Just because your sisters or brothers live closer does not mean they choose to be involved in the practical tasks of caregiving, nor does it mean they have the ability or desire to be responsible and skilled caregivers for your loved one. None of them may want (or agree) to be the primary caregiver. Ideally, your loved one's primary caregiver will be a person who follows God's threefold spiritual calling for caregiving:

to love God, to love neighbor (care recipient), and to love self. So who will be the primary caregiver?

The optimal way to care for your loved one if you live at a distance is for you to be a co-primary caregiver with another family member who lives near your loved one. For example, when the nearby caregiver provides hands-on care, we long-distance caregivers can do the following tasks from afar: telephone our loved one every morning and evening to make sure she is all right, coordinate home health workers via the telephone, contact insurance companies and medical providers, contact transportation services when our loved one has appointments outside the home, handle our loved one's finances, call her church to ask the pastor to make periodic home visits, and provide emotional and spiritual encouragement and support.

Indeed, when we have a willing and capable person with whom to share primary caregiving responsibilities, not only does our loved one receive wonderful care but we also have another person with whom to share our feelings. Remember to periodically hold family conferences (see chapter 7).

Whether out of personal dedication to our loved one or out of necessity, those of us who live a significant geographical distance away can indeed be our loved one's primary caregiver. In fact, nearly 25 percent of long-distance caregivers in the United States are primary caregivers for older relatives or friends.[4] In our hearts, we may know (along with God and our care recipient) that we are the most sensitive, involved, committed, and effective caregivers for our loved ones who need special care at this stage in life.

Do not expect to receive acclaim or gratitude from your siblings when you are the primary caregiver. Humbly go about fulfilling your spiritual caregiving calling to love God, your neighbor (care recipient), and yourself—and when possible love your siblings whether they help you or not.

FEELINGS OF GUILT AND DEPRESSION

We who live a long distance from our care recipient experience many of the same feelings as attentive nearby caregivers. See chapter 4 for descriptions of our feelings and the tips to address them. Our feelings of guilt and depression, however, are more complicated than for those who live near their care recipients.

Guilt. Because we cannot get in our car and immediately be there for our loved one, a constant feeling of guilt is common. We are simply unable to observe and immediately respond to daily changes in our loved one's condition, even though we may telephone our care recipient throughout the day. We also may feel (rightly or wrongly) criticized by our loved one's physicians, home health workers, neighbors, and friends for not being immediately available. Sometimes we even illogically criticize ourselves.

Accept the fact that you cannot always be present for your loved one. Most people (including your loved one) understand the educational, career, and personal choices that resulted in your living at a distance. Rather than beating yourself up about living far away, affirm yourself for the types of care you provide to your loved one from a distance. Rely on God's love and guidance in caring for your loved one and for yourself. Don't lose heart. God loves you and will take care of you.

Depression. Just as guilt leads to feelings of depression, so do other unique circumstances for long-distance caregivers. For example, don't be surprised if you feel depressed in the following situations:

- You regularly telephone your loved one and cannot ascertain how he is feeling, even though you encourage him to describe his feelings and you listen to the inflections in his voice. You become worried.

- Your care recipient reaches the point where he cannot speak or use the telephone because he has suffered a speech impediment due to a stroke, he is too sick to talk, or he is not strong enough to hold the telephone. You have lost your ability to be in relationship with him from afar.

- Your care recipient's vision deteriorates so that she cannot see the cards and flowers you send her, and no one reads her your message or holds the flowers close to her so she can smell their fragrance. You are discouraged and tempted to discontinue sending gifts. Please don't quit. There may come a day when someone will read your card or bring your flowers close to her. On that day your loving heart will touch her heart.

- Your care recipient develops dementia and not only fails to remember that you previously telephoned, sent a birthday card, sent flowers or another gift, or told him you loved him but he also forgets your name and identity. Again, don't give up. As painful as it is, remind him of your name and tell him who you are. Whether it is your voice on the telephone or a gift that you send, the exact moment—even if it is a fleeting moment—when he experiences your love is a special time during which your hearts touch. God is there, making it a poignant moment for both of you.

- Your care recipient's medical condition is more fragile than ever before, but her physician is unable to tell you how close she is to death—whether it is weeks, months, or even a year away. You fear being absent when she dies, but the distance and your job make it impossible for you to be there constantly. Take heart, keep praying for your loved one, make as many contacts with her as possible, and remember, if she dies suddenly, she will not be alone. God will be with her and will also be with you in your sorrow and grief. (See chapters 12 and 13 regarding dying, death, and bereavement.)

When feeling guilty or depressed, please do not question your worth or goodness. Instead, bless yourself for who you are as a beloved child of God and for what you are doing in living out your threefold spiritual caregiving calling from afar. Ease up on yourself. Join a caregiver support group or find a counselor or pastor who is a caring person and a good listener. Regularly refer to chapter 3 in this book for spiritual nurturing tips and chapter 4 for psychological nurturing tips. Take heart and remember that God guides you and God loves you.

FINANCIAL CONCERNS

Long-distance caregivers may incur considerably more financial expenses than nearby family caregivers. Telephone calls, flowers, cards, gifts, postage, automobile expenses for driving to the loved one's home, airplane tickets, hotels, parking fees, and meals in restaurants are just some of your additional expenses. Plus, if your loved one is a person of little financial means, you might pay for all or part of your care recipient's groceries, medications, insurance premiums, home health care fees, and geriatric case management fees. You also might pay for collect telephone calls from your care recipient and others who contact you with caregiving reports. According to a study of long-distance caregivers conducted by MetLife Mature Market Institute,[5] including travel expenses, caregivers who live one to three hours from their care recipient spent an average of $386 per month on caregiving expenses and those living more than three hours away averaged $674 per month.

Long-distance caregiving also indirectly affects your employment income. For instance, you may need to take time off to travel to your loved one's home for a medical emergency. Depending upon the nature of your employment, your absence from work may or may not be paid time off. A leave of absence from work decreases your annual income and adversely affects your personal budget. More than 36 percent of long-distance caregivers report missing days of work, and some of them (especially women) reduce their work status from full time to part time.[6] (Refer back to chapter 2 for tips on dealing with employment issues.)

Additionally, spending vacation time caring for your loved one might mean that the money you saved for a dream vacation will instead be spent on caregiving. Or if you planned to spend your vacation at home in order not to spend money, traveling to your loved one's home—to care for her during this time—means that you will spend money that you preferred not to spend.

In all likelihood, your loved one will understand a lack of funds. If both you and your care recipient cannot afford the cost of caregiving expenses or the cost of long-distance caregiving, ask your loved one if she is willing to consider moving closer to you or living with you.

Chapter 7 includes questions to ask before making the decision to live together. The end of this chapter has additional considerations to factor in when considering moving your care recipient a long distance.

The main thing to remember about finances is that whether or not you have an adequate amount of money to spend as a long-distance caregiver, communicate this message to your loved one: "You are important to me, and I love you."

VISITING YOUR LOVED ONE

Pray. Prior to arriving at your loved one's home for a visit, ask God to help you to be a loving, respectful, and effective long-distance caregiver. If you perceive your loved one's situation differently than he or other family members do, keeping a prayerful focus to your visit will help you avoid a common criticism that long-distance caregivers receive (sometimes accurately; usually unfairly): that you come for a few days and try to change everything. A humble, prayerful focus will help you to remember that even as a long-distance caregiver, your spiritual calling in life is to love God, love your neighbor (care recipient), and love yourself.

Enjoy your time together. When you visit your care recipient, schedule enough time both to enjoy one another's company and to attend to necessary chores. You do not want to have regrets in either area when you return home. In the account of Jesus' visit to Mary and Martha's home (Luke 10:38–42), Martha spent all her time focusing upon household preparations while Mary sat at Jesus' feet and listened to him. When you visit your loved one, do not focus exclusively on things that have to be done. Be assured, you will accomplish them. Instead, be both a Mary and a Martha. As God touches your heart during your visit, touch your loved one's heart and allow him to touch yours. Later, as you look back on your visit, sharing loving time will be your best memory of your time together.

Know what to talk about. Prior to your visit, refer to chapter 5 and appendix D for visitation tips and topics of conversation. Be sure to include the following open-ended questions in your conversations with your loved one so that if they need to be addressed before you return home, you have the time and opportunity to do so:

- "How are you feeling physically?"
- "How are you feeling emotionally?"
- "How are you feeling spiritually?"
- "What do you need help with?"
- "Is there something you need from a store?"
- "What do you want, not just what do you need? A cup of Starbucks coffee? A new shirt? A visit to the cemetery to visit a loved one's grave? To sit in your church's sanctuary to worship or reflect?"
- "How else can I help to make life happier for you?"

Initiate personalized special conversation. Watch family home videos (including videos in which you and your loved one appear) and regularly pause the video so that you can talk about special memories. Look at photo albums together, and reminisce about past experiences. If possible, go for a drive together to a special place from the past—such as a previous home, a favorite park, a favorite scenic location—and talk about the enjoyable memories that arise.

Bring a reminiscence music box. In advance of your visit, prepare a reminiscence music box, so that during your visit, you can show your loved one how to use it. The reminiscence music box is made from a large music box that has an empty compartment or, if you cannot find a large music box, is made from a large decorative box to which you affix a music box. The music is very important because music touches the heart and soul in ways that other forms of communication don't. Select a tune that has a meaningful message for you and your loved one, such as "You Light Up My Life"; "Wind Beneath My Wings"; "You Are My Sunshine"; "Memories" (from *Cats*); "Sunrise, Sunset" (from *Fiddler on the Roof*).

Place special photographs and small pieces of paper—upon which you have written brief descriptions of important experiences that you and your loved one shared in the past—in the empty compartment in the box. For example, you might write on a small piece of paper: "I remember when I had surgery and you sat with me in the hospital and comforted me. You said, 'It's okay to moan. Go ahead and moan if you want to. It will make you feel better.' You were right. I did feel better." Or, "I remember when you were my Girl Scout leader and you taught us how to build a campfire. I learned to cherish God's creation through your love for the outdoors." Or, "I remember the sacrifice you made so that I could have private trumpet lessons. My trumpet was the love of my life at that time."

Invite your loved one to take one item out of the reminiscence music box each day—as she listens to the music—and recall pleasant memories from your life together. You might want to make a duplicate reminiscence music box for yourself so that you also can relive pleasurable experiences from the past.

Throughout your visit, take notes and photographs so that when you return home you can write brief statements about your time together on small pieces of paper. Mail them, along with special photographs from your visit, to your loved one. Invite her to place them in the reminiscence music box and remove one per day as a way of emotionally extending your visit together.

Make observations and evaluations. After you refer to suggestions that are included in chapter 5 for evaluating your loved one's condition, also consider the following suggestions, because they are especially applicable when you travel a long distance to visit your care recipient:

- Schedule an appointment with your loved one and his physician to get an update on his medical condition. Visit with home health workers about his condition. If you observe bruises on your loved one, they can indicate a problem with ambulation, falling, or abuse. Evaluate whether your loved one needs a cane or a walker. Schedule an appointment with his physician to make sure that his tendency to fall is not symptomatic of a more serious medical condition. Ask your loved one about people who may be physically abusing him, such as family members or home health workers.

- Watch for new health problems. If your loved one speaks more loudly than usual, ascertain whether his hearing has deteriorated and needs to be checked. If there is a urine odor in his home, he may have bladder problems and may need to see a physician. If he has body odor, he may not be bathing regularly and may need home health care (or additional hours of home health care). A change in physical appearance (such as not dressing properly, not shaving, not combing his hair, not trimming his fingernails or toe nails, etc.) often indicates physical or mental limitations.

- Observe whether your loved one is more confused than during your last visit. If necessary, make an appointment with her physician for an evaluation of possible memory loss. Keep in mind that confusion and forgetfulness can be caused by verbal abuse inflicted by family members, neighbors, or home health workers. If she has trouble remembering where items are located, label her dresser drawers and cupboards.

- Observe whether the refrigerator and cupboards are stocked with nutritious foods. Bare cupboards indicate a lack of energy to shop, no transportation to get to the supermarket, an inability to carry groceries home, a lack of finances, or an inability to prepare meals. If necessary, make arrangements for a family member, friend, or home health worker to take your loved one shopping or shop for him. Or, if you observe weight loss, he may need daily Meals on Wheels.

- Observe whether the house is tidy and clean, and whether the basement (if there is one) is safe (including the stairway, furnace, hot water heater, and other appliances). If necessary, hire a housekeeper and home repair person.

- Observe whether your care recipient takes her medications properly, pays bills on time, and handles mail appropriately. Your loved one may need to give someone power of attorney or designate a banker or tax preparer to take over these responsibilities.

- Meet with area family caregivers to support and coordinate with them. Meet with your loved one's neighbors, friends, and other relatives to hear their observations about how she is doing. Ask them if they have noticed any behavioral changes, health problems, or safety issues.

SUPPORTING AREA FAMILY CAREGIVERS

If you are a long-distance caregiver who has family members living near your care recipient and compassionately providing good care, make their lives easier by offering support and services from a distance. Periodically telephone them, e-mail them, and send them cards, thanking them for all they do. Failure to stay in touch with them and support them may be interpreted as criticism, lack of interest, or ingratitude. Let them know you appreciate them, if you do. Occasionally enclose a short inspirational or funny story from the newspaper, a magazine, or the Internet; however, do not inundate their mail. Invite them to ventilate their feelings about their caregiving experience. Accept their feelings. Always participate in family conferences via speakerphone when you are unable to be present.

Encourage loving and attentive area family caregivers to care for themselves and (if you have the means) help them to do so. For example, send them money for respite care so they can take a break and enjoy some rest or recreation. Send them gift certificates for visits to a salon, health club, movie, concert, or other activity of interest. Pay for housecleaning services, medical equipment not covered by insurance companies, and unexpected items required for your care recipient. Surprise them with flowers delivered to their door. Do what you can (within your budget) to show your appreciation to those who lovingly and responsibly help your care recipient.

These short statements do wonders with nearby attentive and loving family caregivers: "I appreciate you and value you"; "I love you"; "Make time for yourself." As you speak and write these heartfelt words, you can encourage area caregivers.

EMERGENCIES

One of the most difficult decisions you will face as a long-distance caregiver is to evaluate when your immediate presence is needed. Develop a process for making your evaluation. Evaluating potential emergency situations is difficult because care recipients commonly inaccurately describe what is happening due to the stress they experience. Similar situations may occur when you make a telephone call to check on your loved one and he does not answer.

Help yourself in these situations by keeping copies of your completed Care Recipient Information Form (appendix A) by your telephone, in your computer, in your Palm Pilot, in your office, and in your automobile. On the form are telephone numbers of area family caregivers, your loved one's neighbors and friends, physicians and hospitals, and your loved one's pastor, so that you can ask them to help you assess the situation.

If you believe the emergency is a life or death situation, call 9-1-1. Otherwise, contact some of the above persons to obtain an objective viewpoint before you make travel plans. Providing these persons (in advance) with prepaid telephone cards, your telephone numbers, and your e-mail address, as well as inviting them to call you collect, makes it more likely that they will contact you if a critical situation develops.

When in doubt about what to do, err on the side of love, compassion, and safety—and travel to your loved one's side. Your care recipient will be grateful that you did, and your mind will be put at ease.

TO RELOCATE OR NOT TO RELOCATE

It is tempting for long-distance caregivers—especially those who harbor guilt feelings—to think that the best caregiving solution is to relocate loved ones to their communities and/or homes. Before doing so, however, ask yourself the following question, "For whom would this solution be best: my loved one or me?" Relocation may be more our agenda than our loved one's agenda—simply because it would be more convenient for us. Do not make your decision without discussing with your loved one the crucial evaluative questions listed in chapter 7.

Whenever possible, allow your loved one to remain in his own home. Unless he is a threat to his safety or the safety of another person, allow him to remain where he is, especially if that is his preference. You may need to lower your expectations of how you think he should live his life, such as accepting that he may not clean the house with the same diligence as he did when he was more energetic; he may not prepare the same high-quality meals that he prepared when the food preparation task was easier for him (as long as he continues to eat properly), and he may not socialize as frequently as he did in the past. He may be content with these lifestyle changes. The question is: Can you accept the changes and be content?

On the other hand, if your loved one states that she prefers to move, discuss these questions related to relocating her to your home or community:

- Is your loved one physically able to travel the long distance?

- Is there an assisted-living facility or other care facility in your community that would meet your loved one's needs?

- Will she feel safe in a city and state that may have a different pace of life, such as moving from a rural or suburban area to a fast urban area with a higher crime rate?

- Will she feel comfortable if she moves to a community of broader ethnic diversity?

- Will she miss family members and friends who currently live near her?

- Will she miss her physicians who know her well?

- Will she miss her favorite coffee shop, supermarket, senior citizen center, and other places of significance that she can locate and travel to by herself? Will she feel disoriented because she does not know where anything is located in your community? Will this mean that she has to give up driving an automobile and/or using public transportation, thereby adding to a sense of isolation?

- Will she miss her church where she has been nourished with God's Word for years and where she wants to have her funeral?

Sometimes relocation works well—and other times it is a disaster. On the surface, relocation may seem ideal for both the care recipient and long-distance caregiver. If you mutually decide upon relocation, consider waiting to sell your loved one's house or give a vacancy notice at her apartment building until you know that the new living arrangement works well. Although living in the same community (and possibly in your home) can be the greatest blessing you will share together over the course of your lifetime, it may not work. Give yourselves the option of your loved one's returning to her current housing situation—along with hiring home health care. Trust the Spirit of God to lead you to the best living situation for each of you.

TAKE HEART

Remember, God will give you the strength and guidance to live out your spiritual calling from afar. The suggestions described in this chapter can help you to care for your loved one. Take heart! Don't get down on yourself. Be at peace. You are important to your care recipient and to God—and they love you. Love yourself!

SCRIPTURE

"Do you not know? Have you not heard? The Lord is the everlasting God, the Creator of the ends of the earth. He will not grow tired or weary, and his understanding no one can fathom. He gives strength to the weary and increases the power of the weak. Even youths grow tired and weary, and young men stumble and fall; but those who hope in the Lord will renew their strength. They will soar on wings like eagles; they will run and not grow weary, they will walk and not be faint" (Isaiah 40:28–31).

PRAYER

O God, hear my prayer as I come before you. My loved one who lives far away from me needs our special care. Surround her (him) with your divine comfort, mercy, hope, and peace. Guide me so that I can be a loving and effective caregiver even at this distance—and give me the energy to do so. Helping my loved one is an important part of my spiritual calling, meaning, and purpose in life. Guide all my thoughts, words, and deeds so that I can be a blessing to her (him). Minister to my feelings of guilt for not being there constantly. Fill me with your love, guidance, and peace. In Jesus' name I pray. Amen.

Chapter Ten
Celebrating Holidays and Birthdays

Holidays and birthdays are heartwarming special occasions through which we have additional opportunities to live out our spiritual caregiving calling. Through them we lovingly touch our loved one's heart with ours—and God deeply touches both of us.

Do you cherish spending these special times with your loved one as I do? I look forward to them and eagerly anticipate them. I want to make these occasions very special for Mom—and for me. I savor each opportunity. When we remember the spiritual meaning of each event—and talk about it with our loved ones—these occasions are blessings for them and for us. For example:

- As we give thanks to God for sending His Son Jesus into the world at Christmas, let's remind our care recipient and ourselves that through Jesus' human nature, he understands our care recipient's daily struggles and our daily caregiving challenges; and through his divine nature, Jesus shares with each of us his strength, compassion, and hope.

- As we give thanks to God at Easter for raising Jesus from the dead, let's talk with our care recipient about the comforting promise of eternal life made possible through the cross and resurrection of Jesus Christ. Let's rejoice that through faith in Christ our place is assured in eternity and that one day we will be reunited before the throne of God.

- As we give thanks to God on Pentecost Sunday for the gift of the Holy Spirit, we can talk with our care recipient about the Spirit's role in creating, nourishing, and sustaining our faith.

- As we celebrate Thanksgiving Day, we can talk about the blessings that God has given us in past years, continues to give us in the present, and promises to give us in all the days and years ahead. (Also review the section about caregiver blessings found in chapter 3.)

Follow the same prayerful thought processes for other holidays and special occasions. For example, on New Year's Day give thanks for new beginnings, on Memorial Day give thanks to God for your relatives and friends who died in the faith, and on Mother's Day and Father's Day thank and honor your parents for making personal sacrifices for you (or remember the ones they made for you).

The tendency of many caregivers on holidays and birthdays is to focus more upon the preparations for the special day than upon their relationship with their care recipient. This can happen because special occasions require extra physical and mental energy. God will give us the guidance and strength to meet our challenges. Rather than ignoring important occasions, thinking that your loved one is not aware of them, instead, focus upon your relationship with your loved one and create new memories. As you do so, ask God to fill your heart with a deeper love for your care recipient.

HOLIDAY CHALLENGES AND TIPS TO MEET THEM

The more prepared you are for dealing with holiday challenges, the better you will be able to enjoy the special occasion as a blessing from God. The following list of challenges and tips to address them may help.

Feelings of grief. As you recall past holidays and birthdays that were happier and simpler than they are now, you grieve because you know these occasions will never be the same again—due to your loved one's limitations and your own lower energy level. It is also common to sadly wonder if this will be your loved one's last holiday or birthday before she dies. Share your feelings of grief with a trusted person and with God in prayer. Giving voice to your grief alleviates some of your loneliness and mobilizes you to modify this year's plans. Open your heart to God and experience his love and peace so that you don't get discouraged during these special times.

Modified plans. As you and your loved one modify your plans, ask yourselves, "What are our goals for the special day?" As you formulate your goals, ask yourselves:

- Do we want a quiet day that requires only a few preparations?

- Do we want to invite a lot of family members and friends, even though extensive preparations will be necessary?

- If we limit the attendance, whom do we want to invite because we enjoy their company the most?

- Which family traditions can we still maintain this year and what new (and simpler) traditions do we want to begin?

- If we attend outside events, how many events will we attend? Base your decision upon your loved one's health, who will be there, and what you will be expected to bring that requires an additional expenditure of time, energy, and money (such as refreshments and gifts). It's perfectly fine to attend only one event.

Since your daily caregiving tasks are difficult enough, modify your plans so that both you and your loved one can enjoy the special occasion. In other words, downsize the event to fit your best interests and capabilities.

Traveling with your loved one. If your loved one is able to travel, these tips may alleviate some of the stress of traveling:

- Help your loved one pack her suitcase. She may be relieved to receive your assistance, and you can see that all essential items are packed. Remember to include medications, medical equipment, and special foods.

- Carry a copy of the Care Recipient Information Form found in appendix A. If you have transferred that information to your laptop computer, take your laptop. Also carry a copy of your loved one's power of attorney and durable power of attorney for health care forms.

- Expect problems to occur.

- If you travel to a large gathering, leave one day early to allow your loved one to rest before the event.

- If you fly, hire a skycap to help you maneuver through the airport. If you drive a long distance, stop every hour for a break.

- Request a handicap-friendly hotel room with handrails by the toilet and in the shower. Inquire whether hotel restaurants and other public areas are handicap-accessible.

- Encourage your loved one to eat as normally as possible rather than trying new foods that may cause gastrointestinal distress.

- Do not expect your loved one to stay for the entire length of the event. It may be too strenuous.

- If your loved one becomes upset at the event, be calm and find a quiet area in which she can relax. If necessary, leave the event.

Gift suggestions for care recipients and caregivers. Many special occasions involve gifts for your care recipient. Remember that the price of a gift is not what gives it its value. Its value comes from the giver. Remind yourself and others who ask for gift suggestions that spending quality time together may be the most cherished gift your loved one receives. Some of the following gifts may be particularly appropriate for your loved one:

- An unrushed daily or weekly visit
- A daily telephone call

- A daily prayer

- Running errands

- Doing weekly laundry and housecleaning

- Doing paper work

- A weekly ride to church

- A drive to a favorite place

- A weekly hand or foot massage (including nail trimming). (See chapter 5 for massage directions.)

- Gift certificates for haircuts, hair styling, Meals on Wheels, groceries, pharmacy items, snow shoveling, lawn mowing, an emergency alert system, and restaurants

- Family pictures

- A family video

- A large-print Bible, large-print books, and large-print crossword puzzles

- A newspaper or magazine subscription

- A prepaid long-distance telephone card

- An extension telephone by the bed, a cordless telephone, or a jumbo-numbered telephone

- A large-numbered wristwatch, clock, or calculator

- A basket for a walker or a carrying bag for a wheelchair

- A monthly bouquet of fresh flowers or a flowering plant

- Paying winter heating bills and summer air-conditioning bills

- A basket of favorite toiletries, including deodorant, toothpaste, mouthwash, bubble bath, shampoo, hair conditioner, aftershave lotion, perfume, hand lotion, and sachets

- A basket of favorite homemade goodies, such as cookies, breads, muffins, and other family recipes

- Books of stamps and all-occasion cards
- Equipment listed in chapter 6
- Regularly hearing the words "I love you!"

Sometimes your care recipient, other family members, and friends also ask for gift suggestions for *you*. Unless you have something specific you'd like, consider suggesting the following ideas for yourself:

- A gift certificate at a spa for a massage, manicure, pedicure, and/or hair styling
- A gift certificate for respite hours or home health care services hours
- A gift certificate for prepared meals brought to the home once per week (such as Sunday dinners), once per month, or at other designated times.
- A gift certificate to a video/DVD rental store or a paid monthly subscription to an Internet movie rental site
- Tickets to a favorite event along with plans for someone to care for your loved one while you are out
- A gift certificate for a weekend at a favorite hotel along with arrangements for respite care
- A daily prayer

Visitors. Although contact with family and friends is important for you and your care recipient during holidays and birthdays, request that visitors telephone before they come to visit. Inquire whether they have a cold or a cough. If they do, request that they wait until they are well before they visit. If your loved one is ill or has had more people visiting with him that day than he could handle and enjoy, request that they visit another day. When it is appropriate for your loved one to have company, advise visitors about behavioral or cognitive changes that have occurred since their last visit and share helpful tips for how to communicate with your loved one.

Keep in mind that family members who only visit on special occasions are sometimes in denial about your care recipient's deterioration and unable to face the daily problems inherent in your loved one's condition. (This is true also, however, for family members who visit frequently for very short periods of time and do not pay attention to problems.) These persons may act out their frustration and sadness by challenging your assessment of the situation and the arrangements you have made for care. As a way of sharing information, experiences, and thoughts, offer to hold a family conference before they return to their own homes. (See chapter 7 regarding recommended guidelines and an agenda for family conferences.)

Self-care. Caring for yourself is a greater challenge during the holidays and birthdays than during your regular caregiving days. Do not fool yourself into thinking you don't have time to take care of yourself. Review chapters 3 and 4 for important spiritual and psychological self-care suggestions. Here are additional tips for holidays and birthdays:

- Rather than doing a lot of baking and cooking, pay someone to make your favorite recipes, use a bakery, or hire a caterer.

- Rather than expending energy at shopping centers, purchase presents from catalogs or over the Internet.

- If you spend a night decorating the Christmas tree, have pizza delivered and enjoy your Christmas lights.

- Take time to laugh and enjoy being with your loved one.

- Take time to do nothing but listen to holiday music together.

- Do something you like to do, even if it involves paying for respite care.

Due to your additional caregiving challenges, lower your expectations. Accept the fact that holiday and birthday plans will not be carried out perfectly and that you will not always handle your stress well. Unavoidable incidents will occur. When they do, maintain your sense of humor and adapt to the new situation. Don't lose sight of how spiritually meaningful your special occasion is.

BIRTHDAYS AND "BLESSING OF A BIRTHDAY PROGRAM"

Before my mother celebrated her eightieth birthday, I knew that I wanted to make it an extra special event with wonderful memories. I felt so blessed to still have Mom with me. Considering all the medical problems and emotional stress my mother has experienced (and continues to undergo in life), having her reach eighty years of age was about the deepest blessing I could receive from God. I planned and planned—and prayed and prayed—about how to make her birthday a very special time for her.

One of the main challenges I faced in planning her birthday celebration was that Mom said she did not want a large gathering of people. For a variety of reasons, Mom gets nervous when there are a lot of people around. I knew that if Mom was going to enjoy her birthday, I needed to respect her wishes.

Out of my thankfulness to Mom for all she has done for me, I wrote the "Blessing of a Birthday Program." This service came from deep within my heart. On the day of her birthday, it was very touching as we (Mom, my brother and his wife and daughter [Mom's only grandchild], and I) went through it sitting in her balloon- and banner-decorated living room. It was so touching for me that I had to fight back tears as my heart touched Mom's heart.

Prior to the program I prepared one of Mom's favorite meals—barbequed ribs with the works and birthday cake with candles—and after the program we surprised Mom with a concert in her living room performed by her favorite area vocalist and musician (whom she knew from church), who set up his guitar and speakers. He serenaded Mom with some of her favorite songs and hymns. Through music, God blessed all of us with joy and happiness and peace. The private concert ended with all of us singing "Happy Birthday." After the program, when Mom and I were alone, I gave her presents.

I commend my "Blessing of a Birthday Program" (outlined below) to you. Celebrate your loved one's birthday with heartfelt love and affection. Whether you plan a public birthday party, a small gathering of family members or friends, or a party just for the two of you, make this occasion extra special by including this program. Modify the program to fit your situation and add special touches that will be especially meaningful for all of you. For example, you might want to add:

- A photo collage of your loved one with special people and during important events in her life
- A memory album including written statements from special people in her life
- Songs sung by family members (including grandchildren) or played on their musical instruments
- Short speeches by significant persons, such as friends and family members who share their warm feelings of love and gratitude with your loved one
- A special message by your loved one's pastor
- The reading of birthday cards from those who are unable to attend the celebration. These are people dear to your loved one, whom you contact in advance. (I contacted relatives in advance of Mom's eightieth birthday, asking them to send her cards. She enjoyed receiving them in the days leading up to her birthday.)

Blessing of a Birthday Program

Happy birthday, _____, and may God bless you today and in all the years to come. We, your family and friends, love you and thank you for your love and care for us all these years. You are a gift that grows more valuable and cherished in our hearts and lives every day. May God, who loves and fills your life with meaning and joy, be with you on this special occasion of your _____ birthday!

We read in Leviticus 19:32, "Rise in the presence of the aged, show respect for the elderly and revere your God." Reverence to God and to those who are older than us is part of our Christian faith. Today as we celebrate your birthday, we want you to know that we revere, respect, and value you as one who was created in God's image and proclaimed to be very good! You are, and have always been, a true reflection of sacrificial Christian love for us.

Today we celebrate the day when you were born and God gave you as a gift to your parents, to your brothers and sisters, and to the world. We—your children, grandchildren, nieces, nephews, and friends—are very blessed to call you _____ and _____. Your birthday is a special time when we celebrate and give thanks for the gifts of love and joy that you have shared with us.

We, your children, are blessed with your physical attributes, your special traits, virtues, values, faith, and the intangible gifts that you have given to us—gifts such as your affection, love, joy, laughter, sacrifice, and companionship. You give our lives meaning and purpose. We cherish you. You are important to us.

We thank you for these fond childhood memories:

- (For example:) Your emphasis on cleanliness, as you made sure we were clean (our bodies, our hair, our clothes, and our language)

- Your assistance with our homework

- Your desire that we enjoy a good Christmas every year. We especially remember the year you had Santa Claus visit us at home because all of us children had the chicken pox.

- (Other memories special to your family)

We thank you for your special traits that we also strive to emulate:

- (For example:) Living life to the fullest

- When faced with challenges, solving them rather than giving up

- Enduring suffering and not giving in to it

- (Other traits or qualities particular to your loved one)

We thank you for your special talents and interests:

- (For example:) Your delicious home cooking and baking
- Your knack for growing gladiolas and tomatoes
- Your interest and skill in learning how to use the computer, including the Internet, at age seventy-six
- (Other talents and interests particular to your loved one)

We thank you for the special blessings you share with your grandchildren:

- (For example:) Playing dolls, playing school, drawing and coloring together, playing softball and volleyball
- Loving them and giving them hugs
- Sharing your faith and wisdom with them
- (Other blessings and values your loved one has shared)

We thank you for these special lessons of faith that you shared with us:

- (For example:) Teaching us how to pray and saying table and bedtime prayers with us
- Being reverent in our home and taking us to church every Sunday to learn to love and worship God
- Reading your Bible every day, memorizing Bible verses, and underlining special verses
- (Other practices or lessons of faith particular to your loved one)

Today as we celebrate your _____ birthday, we celebrate and honor you. You are a blessing to each of us. You are our special angel! Your wisdom guides and supports us in times of happiness, joy, discouragement, pain, and loss. Your laughter touches us with rays of sunshine from your warm heart of love. We thank you that you have used your gift of years to bless our years.

We honor you with our love. We are proud that you are our _____ _____ and _____. We only hope that we can follow in your footsteps to make the world around us a better place in which to live, just as you make it a better place for us. May good things and beautiful dreams, and our love and God's love, make your heart overflow with happiness and peace, today and every day.

A reading from Isaiah 43:1–4:

"But now, this is what the Lord says—he who created you . . . he who formed you . . . 'Fear not, for I have redeemed you; I have [called] you by name _____; you are mine. When you pass through the waters, I will be with you; and when you pass through the rivers, they will not sweep over you. . . . For I am the Lord, your God, the Holy One of Israel, your Savior. . . . You are precious and honored in my sight . . . I love you.' "

Let us pray: Our gracious God, we give you thanks for the blessing of years that you have given to our precious _____ and _____. You created her and molded her in your image, as her parents raised her in the Christian faith. At this time of her special birthday, we thank and praise you for the life she has given us. We thank you that she raised us in the faith so that we will be close to you all our lives, just as she is close to you. With loving hearts and lighted candles, we celebrate her life. Continue to bless her with your presence. Fill her with your wisdom. Bestow upon her your strength and surround her with your love so that each day of her life is filled with happiness, contentment, and peace. Through Jesus Christ we pray, amen.

Receive the benediction: And now may the Lord bless you and keep you. The Lord make his face shine upon you and be gracious to you. The Lord look upon you with favor and give you peace. In the name of the Father and of the Son and of the Holy Spirit. Amen. (From Numbers 6:24–26.)

We love you, _____, and share these tender hugs with you! God bless you!

SCRIPTURE

"Give thanks to the Lord, for he is good; his love endures forever" (Psalm 107:1).

PRAYER

O God, my loved one and I (and our family) have had wonderful holidays and birthdays together in the past. Now, due to my loved one's limitations, I am unsure if I can handle preparing for this occasion. My memories of the past are tender and I grieve the wonderful experiences from past years with her (him). It just isn't the same anymore. Help me to relate to my loved one with deep love and a positive attitude. Let me keep a spiritual perspective on this special occasion and upon our relationship. I pray that this holiday (or birthday) will be a time to cherish forever, as we create new and tender memories. Bless us with your love and peace. In Jesus' name I pray. Amen.

Chapter Eleven
Nursing Homes, Assisted-Living Facilities, and Other Care Facilities

It is a tender moment when you and your care recipient discuss whether she needs to live in a nursing home, assisted-living facility, or other care facility. The idea of relocation after many years of living independently, perhaps in the same home, brings forth mixed emotions. Both of you share feelings of loss and grief over your loved one's deteriorating health. Both of you also feel anxious as you speculate what your loved one's life (and yours) might be like in a care facility. As you consider relocation, remember that God is always with you. He guides you and loves you as you ponder your decision. Take heart and be at peace.

DETERMINING FACTORS FOR RELOCATION

How do you decide if a care facility is needed? First, assess your care recipient's medical condition. Second, evaluate your ability to provide adequate care. Ask yourself the following questions about your *care recipient*:

- Does your loved one remember to take her medication, take it in the correct amount, and take it at the proper times?
- Is her frequency of falling increasing so that she is at high risk for serious injury?
- Is she able to shop for groceries or obtain them in other ways?

Is she able and willing to make or obtain nutritious meals for herself? Does she need assistance with eating?

- Is she frightened to be alone at night?

- Is she able to manage her urinary or fecal incontinence?

- Does she wander away from home, confused about where she is?

- Is she isolated from people? Does she need socialization opportunities?

Now ask yourself the following questions about *your* ability to *provide* care:

- Are you burned out from physical exhaustion, lack of sleep, compromised family relationships, or the everyday tasks of caregiving and dealing with your loved one's psychological concerns and confusion?

- Are you able to obtain all the necessary levels of home health care?

- Have you developed a physical handicap, disease, or other medical condition (such as cancer, stroke, or fibromyalgia) that makes it impossible to continue to provide care?

- Has your work performance suffered due to the strain of caregiving to the point that in order to continue to finan-cially support yourself as well as contribute to your loved one's support you can no longer engage in your current level of caregiving?

While it is imperative to evaluate your loved one's ability to care for herself, do not minimize the toll caregiving takes on you. The National Family Caregivers Association reports that nursing home placement is more often the result of caregiver burnout than the care recipient's medical needs.[1] Thus the decision about relocation may be based more upon your needs than hers.

APPROACHING YOUR LOVED ONE ABOUT THE NEED TO RELOCATE TO A CARE FACILITY

If possible, begin the conversation with your care recipient about assisted-living or nursing home placement *before* it is necessary to relocate. The early discussion will enable both of you to talk about it more objectively. It is easier to keep raw emotions out of such a conversation when you are not at a point of needing to make an immediate decision. Later, if a crisis occurs, you will have followed the tips in this chapter and will be ready to act.

If your loved one is resistant to the idea of one day relocating to a care facility, be a compassionate listener. Acknowledge his feelings and let him know that if such a move becomes necessary, it will be emotionally difficult for you also. Moving a loved one out of his home to a care facility can be one of the most heartbreaking decisions a family makes. It often involves leaving a place of security and deep memories. In a care facility, your loved one would experience even more losses than he does now, including the inability to set his own schedule and to make his own decisions. As you actively listen, share your personal feelings of anticipatory grief and sorrow with your loved one. Don't try to be stoic. Let your hearts touch. Remember also to share your mutual feelings with God in prayer.

After you have followed the tips in this chapter for selecting your mutually preferred care facility, decide together whether to place your loved one's name on the waiting list of your first- and second-choice homes. Being on the waiting list does not obligate your care recipient to accept a room if the facility notifies him that one is available. He can always decline the room and request to remain at the top of the admissions list. If, on the other hand, he does not apply in advance for admission to his preferred home, when an emergency occurs (for example, debilitating stroke, a broken hip, a severe eye problem resulting in loss of vision) he will not be on the admissions list and may have to relocate elsewhere due to lack of an available room.

If placement is necessary at this time and your loved one is resistant, ask his physician or home health care supervisor to discuss with

Facilities

cal reasons for relocation. If possible, honor your loved
g him time to adjust to the relocation decision before he
, to move. Assure him that he is important to you, that
yo͟   ͟sit him in the new home with the same frequency you do
now, and that you will continue to help him in all the ways that you
can—because you love him.

HOW TO SELECT A FACILITY

The best way to find out about the quality of a facility is by word
of mouth. Knowing two or more family caregivers whose loved ones
enjoy living in a particular facility that provides high-quality care is a
powerful recommendation. Try not to base your decision upon only one
person's viewpoint. Sometimes pastors are willing to suggest facilities
that their members and families appreciate. Pastors also might caution you about sub-par facilities where they have visited parishioners.
Consider all the options for the new living situation: assisted-living
facilities, Continuing Care Retirement Centers (CCRCs), nursing
homes (including church-related homes and Eden Alternative homes),
and board-and-care homes.

Overall quality of care. Select only a licensed facility, because
it is required to comply with quality care guidelines established by the
state and federal governments. Since many states do not yet have licensing requirements for assisted-living facilities, you may need to do even
more research about them. Unlicensed facilities are more prone to sub-
par care.

Inspection reports. Read the annual state and federal inspection
(survey) report that should be readily visible and available in every
nursing home. If you cannot find the report, ask the office to find it for
you. Consult *www.medicare.gov* regarding survey results. This Web site
has valuable information that can help you avoid a home with serious
deficiencies (e.g., lack of proper charting, medication disbursement
problems, safety issues, privacy concerns, poor medical response to
emergencies) in quality of care.

National alerts. Search the Internet for national alerts that may
have been issued about the facilities of interest to you. Such alerts indi-

cate serious infractions of government-mandated quality care regulations. These infractions put residents at risk.

Occupancy rate. Inquire about the occupancy rate. A low rate can indicate problems in the facility.

Even when you receive a positive recommendation for a possible new home for your loved one, do your homework. Evaluate as many of the following factors as possible.

Medical care:

- Does the facility have an in-house physician? How frequently do residents receive physical examinations? Is a registered nurse always on duty in the building, including during overnight hours, weekends, and holidays? What is the ratio of direct-care staff to residents on each shift? At the beginning of shift changes, are nursing assistants given updated information about the residents for whom they provide care? How?

- Does the facility serve residents who need intravenous feeding, tube feeding, dialysis, and ventilators? What safeguards are in place to ensure proper medication management?

- Does the facility have a locked Alzheimer's unit? If not, will your loved one be required to transfer to a different facility if she develops behavior-changing dementia? If the facility has an Alzheimer's unit, what training does the staff on the unit receive? Does the overall nursing staff (including nurse's aides) receive training in dementia issues beyond the basic one-time certified nursing assistant education?

- Will staff persons who work with your loved one speak her language so they can communicate with one another?

- What is the facility's philosophy and practice regarding the use of restraints to control behavior and prevent falls? Will the facility consult with you prior to implementing medication or physical restraints so that you can approve or disapprove of their use?

- How are medical emergencies handled? In an emergency, will the staff contact you immediately?

- Under what circumstances might your loved one be required to leave the facility? If her money runs out? If her physical or mental health deteriorates? If she hits another resident? How much advance notice is given when this occurs? Would you be given a choice regarding where she would go from there?

Walk through the building and make the following observations (you may also want to inquire about some of them):

- What is your first impression? Do you want to flee or stay? (Remember, décor and size do not determine quality of care.)

- Do the residents look happy and clean? Do residents who attend activities look like they want to be there? What are the residents who do not attend activities doing? Are they abandoned in front of public televisions, not knowing where they are?

- When working with residents, do staff members focus their attention upon them or do they talk with one another, ignoring the residents? Does the staff talk down to residents and treat them like children?

- Does the staff (including nursing, housekeeping, and maintenance personnel) give the residents as much privacy as possible, such as knocking on the door to receive the resident's permission to enter? Are medications disbursed in private areas rather than in public locations (such as hallways and dining rooms)? Are medical procedures carried out with residents' room doors closed or open? Do residents sit in hallways in skimpy nightclothes waiting for a bath?

- What sounds do you hear? Do carts squeak, staff persons talk loudly with each other, residents moan and yell, and overhead pages continually disturb? Is it too noisy for residents to rest? Make sure you visit during nighttime hours also, to ascertain if the facility is quiet enough for sleep, as well as to observe the ratio of staff to residents.

- Does the building appear to be clean? Is there a urine or feces odor? Such an odor is (in large part) unnecessary.

- Does the facility have rehabilitation and occupational therapy departments? Is the equipment up-to-date, safe, and always attended by a staff person? Do you see any residents abandoned in a therapy room? What qualifications do the therapists hold? Have they received advanced training beyond basic one-time nursing assistant education?

- Do you see safety issues, such as hallways cluttered with medical carts and equipment, no handrails for residents to use or handrails located too high on the wall for wheelchair residents, chairs without sturdy arm rests (that help with sitting and rising) in the dining room, or poorly maintained wheelchairs? Do you smell noxious odors from cleaning solutions or mold?

- Do you smell smoke? Are residents allowed to smoke in their rooms? If so, are they attended by a staff person? Are staff persons allowed to smoke in the building? Do you smell smoke from their clothing and hair?

- Does the facility have a security alarm system that prevents residents with dementia from wandering out of the building or leaving when visitors enter or exit the building?

- If you are receiving a tour from a staff member, are you being rushed? Is the staff person showing you only areas she wants you to see? Is she purposely attempting to prevent you from seeing a certain area that might be a red flag? Does she have a rapport with the residents or tenants? If she does not seem to care about them, she may not care about your loved one either.

Finances:

- What does the monthly fee include? Request a copy of the prorated fee schedule based upon the number of services your loved one needs. Are additional fees charged for haircuts, special meals, assistance getting to facility chapel services, and transportation to medical appointments outside the facility? Can fees for medical care be reevaluated on a monthly basis, per your loved one's changing needs? His condition might improve so that he needs less care.

- Is it necessary to sign a contract or lease? If so, what does it say about services, costs, and staffing?

- Are private rooms available? How is one obtained? How much more does one cost?

- Do rooms near the elevator, dining room, or nurses' station cost more? If the facility is a high-rise building that has a beautiful view, do units on the upper floors cost more on the choice side of the building?

- Is a leave of absence (beyond the usual number of allocated days for not being in the facility) permitted without losing one's room assignment? If so, are any fees waived?

- Does the facility offer a way to safeguard money and small valuables for the residents? Your loved one should keep only a few dollars (and no valuables) in the room.

- Is the facility a church-related home or an Eden Alternative home? See the next sections in this chapter about the advantages of selecting such homes.

Other:

- Sample the food for all three meals. Observe the residents eating their meals. Are they enjoying the food? Are they offered choices? What safety measures are taken to ensure that special dietary requirements are met and that residents do not choke?

- Does the Activities Department offer activities for higher functioning residents as well as those with low cognitive function?

- Does the facility have a beauty/barber shop? How does one obtain an appointment and how is one transported to it? Is it difficult (or even impossible) for new residents to obtain appointments?

- Are massages, manicures, and pedicures available? What are the fees?

- Does the facility accommodate residents who like to get up late in the morning and stay up late at night?

- How does the facility support the families of residents? Does it have an active Family Council? Are caregiver and bereavement support groups available? Are family caregiving programs offered on topics of interest?

CHURCH-RELATED HOMES

If faith is important to you and to your loved one, consider selecting a facility that has a chaplaincy staff and a self-contained chapel with stationary chapel furnishings (not a makeshift chapel in another room).

Before deciding which church-related home you prefer, visit with the chaplain. Find out if she or he is an ordained pastor or a layperson. Ask what denomination the chaplain is, because this gives an indication of whether the chaplain's religious beliefs are congruent with the institution's affiliation, your loved one's beliefs, and your beliefs. Inquire whether the chaplain has received specific training in geriatric ministry and whether she or he attends continuing education events in this area. Find out if the chaplain is full time or part time and whether there is a secretary to help her or him. Part-time chaplains (and especially those with no secretarial help) are usually overworked and have little time for visitation. Such pastors are primarily liturgical chaplains who only have time for preparing for chapel services and Bible studies, leading those religious events, and (hopefully) visiting residents who are dying. Also ask the chaplain whether her or his job description includes working in disciplines and activities outside the realm of pastoral care that take time away from the spiritual nurture of residents.

Prior to selecting a church-related home, also view the chapel. If a church-related home has no chapel in which residents can pray quietly in private throughout the day (without interruption or extraneous noise), spirituality is not valued in the home. If faith is important to your loved one, make sure he has a special place to be alone and at peace with God—just as was true in his own home. The chapel can also be a place of refuge for you when you come to visit—because sometimes the stress of visiting a loved one in a care facility becomes overwhelming and you need a place where you can get away and regroup before returning to your loved one's room. This is also a common experience for caregivers whose loved ones are in the dying process.

When you tour church-related facilities, ask staff members the following question: "What makes this facility a church-related home, other than having a chaplain, a chapel, and a denominational connection in its constitution or bylaws?" Their answers will give you an indication as to whether only the chaplain relates to residents from a faith perspective or whether the administration encourages the entire staff to do so.

The overall atmosphere in a Christian home should lift up the value of aging persons and honor them with dignity and respect. The staff should be trained to know that just because the physical or mental condition of residents has diminished, they are not less valuable. Just as you relate to your loved one with love, honor, respect, and dignity, the staff in a church-related home should do the same so that your loved one receives Christlike, positive encouragement twenty-four hours per day, seven days a week.

If your loved one moves into a church-related facility, share the following points of information[2] with the chaplain: name, denomination, and address of your loved one's congregation and pastor; types of church activities in which your loved one previously participated; the length of time since your loved one attended worship services regularly; whether he wants to attend chapel worship services, and if he needs assistance getting there; whether he can see to read large-print hymnals and is strong enough to hold them; his favorite hymns; whether he prefers wine or grape juice for Communion; whether he has a hearing problem and needs to sit near a loudspeaker; and whether he wants to attend Bible studies.

Keep in mind one more thing about a church-related home. Although the facility has a chaplain, the chaplain does not replace your loved one's pastor; therefore, inform your loved one's congregation when he moves into a facility. His parish pastor remains his primary spiritual care provider. The chaplain supplements the congregation's ministry. Your loved one needs to know that his congregation and pastor continue to care about him. His parish pastor should visit him with the same frequency in his new home as he did in his previous home. The combination of your loved one's congregational ministry and the facility's pastoral care will help him to know that God's love and peace are always with him.

EDEN ALTERNATIVE HOMES

If your loved one needs a supervised living situation, yet both of you shudder at the idea of institutionalization, consider an Eden Alternative home. Eden Alternative homes are the up-and-coming new form of long-term care—and one day may replace traditional nursing homes.

Dr. Bill Thomas, an impassioned geriatrician, founded the Eden Alternative movement in 1991. Taking its name from the biblical garden in the book of Genesis, Eden homes create an enlivened environment that includes plants, animals, and children. In Eden Alternative homes, the organizational hierarchy treats the staff the way they want the staff to treat the elders—with honor and respect. Loving companionship, opportunities to help others, and meaningful activities are antidotes to loneliness and boredom in these wonderful homes. Residents, family caregivers, and staff are invited to participate in decision making as they strive to help one another experience meaning and purpose in life.

A partial list of Eden Alternative homes is included on their Web site (*www.edenalt.com*). Keep in mind that some church-related care facilities are currently adopting the Eden Alternative philosophy, either in totality or in part. The thought of moving to this new and creative type of eldercare should not make either you or your loved one shudder.

OTHER TYPES OF CARE FACILITIES

CCRC (Continuing Care Retirement Center). These facilities include the following multiple levels of care in the same retirement center: independent living apartments, assisted living, skilled nursing, and dementia care. If your loved one chooses to live in a Continuing Care Retirement Center, as her medical and psychological needs change, she can remain in the same facility—in the most appropriate level of care for her. She also can go back and forth between the types of living situations, as needed. For example, if she breaks a bone and temporarily needs more highly supervised care, she can move to that level of care, and later (when she recovers) return to the previous level of care.

Many CCRCs require a substantial entrance fee as well as a monthly fee. The large fee ensures that continuum life care will be provided for the tenant by the facility on any level. In order to guarantee the continuum of care, some CCRCs require that persons function independently and be healthy when they are admitted. People pay for services they currently need as well as pay to reserve more extensive services, which they may or may not need in the future. This type of living situation is usually an option only for middle- and upper-income people. CCRCs have attractive dining rooms in which apartment tenants and guests can eat, on-campus and off-campus activities, church services, and cultural opportunities.

Senior apartments. These apartments are generally for persons 55 and above, although some require tenants to be 62 years of age. Senior apartments enable older persons to spend their retirement in a community with other people their age. There are low-income senior apartments as well as more expensive ones.

Some senior apartments have communal areas for socializing, community fitness centers with fitness equipment, recreational areas, and dining areas. Some have congregate dining provided by an outside organization. If your loved one applies for a senior apartment and needs a handicap-accessible unit, specifically request it—because not all senior apartments are so equipped.

The difference between senior apartments and assisted-living centers is that those who live independently in senior apartments need to be able to perform their own activities of daily living without help from others. If personal services are needed, seniors must be able to find and coordinate home health providers.

Board-and-care facilities (sometimes called senior group homes, adult foster care, retirement homes, or independent living facilities). These facilities provide a group living situation for individuals who need assistance with the activities and personal care needs of daily living. Some specialize in care for the elderly or for those with physical disabilities, Alzheimer's, or psychiatric problems.

Some board-and-care homes are licensed, but many are not. If you select an unlicensed home, know that without licensure such homes may have untrained or poorly trained staff. This can result in poor nutrition, inattention to medical problems, and neglect of the changing health needs of residents. Without licensure and government-established standards for care, if problems arise, you have no certification or licensure body to which to report them.

If you select this type of housing, ask detailed questions about medical care. Inquire if licensed medical professionals (such as registered nurses or certified nurse assistants) work there—and if they do, whether a licensed physician supervises them. Also ask whether the staff is allowed to administer medications. Some homes cannot allow the staff to do this because the staff does not have the necessary qualifications. This is problematic, because the disbursement of medications is one of the primary reasons people move to a care facility. Also inquire if they have a procedure for responding to the medical needs of the residents. Do they transport and attend a resident who needs to go to a physician's office, urgent care center, emergency room, or hospital? Some board-and-care homes just call an ambulance and the resident goes alone. You would probably not want this to happen to your loved one.

Board-and-care homes tend to be small (usually fewer than ten residents) and less expensive than higher-quality care facilities, yet some house as many as 150 persons. Often the homes are located in residential areas. Many have shared living room space, dining rooms, bedrooms, and bathrooms. As such, there is little privacy either for your loved one or for you when you visit.

Memory loss centers (also called Alzheimer's units or dementia care units). These centers are usually located within a nursing home. They provide all-around personal safety and trained supervision for those with impaired memory. The architectural design contributes to security both inside the unit and on the grounds. If your loved one needs to relocate to a memory loss center, the key questions to ask are: "Does the staff have advanced training in dementia beyond the basic nursing assistant course?" and "Does the staff receive frequent continuing education about caring for persons with memory loss?"

Hospices. See chapter 12 for information about these wonderful centers that care for your loved one who has been given a prognosis of less than six months to live or who has chosen not to seek curative treatment for a terminal condition. Hospices provide exceptionally wonderful supportive care to families as well.

TIPS FOR VISITING IN A CARE FACILITY

When visiting your loved one, do so in a manner worthy of your threefold spiritual caregiving calling. Just as God touches your heart when you visit, your heart touches the hearts of everyone around you. Be loving, kind, affirming, and patient. Let your loved one and the staff say this about you after each visit: "I always look forward to her visits because she loves everyone and makes me feel good about myself."

Visitation schedule. How often do you want to visit your loved one? There is no right or wrong answer. Base the frequency of your visits upon your loved one's changing needs as well as your own. At times it is beneficial to take a day off from visiting so that you can care for yourself and do things you enjoy. When you do so, your time with your loved one will be more pleasurable for both of you.

Allow adequate time for each visit so that your loved one does not feel rushed when talking with you. He needs more time to think about what he wants to say—and how to say it—than you do. Honor him by scheduling ample time for the visit. Sometimes just sit and enjoy being together without speaking.

It is a good idea to inform your loved one that you are coming to visit on a specific date and at a specific time. When you give him advance notice of your visit, he will have something to look forward to. But you may also want to arrive unannounced occasionally to ensure that the staff does not base the quality of care they provide for him upon your presence or absence. Vary your visiting schedule so that you can observe how the staff cares for him at different times of the day and different days of the week, including evenings, nights, and weekends. It is common that residents whose family caregivers regularly visit receive better care.

When possible, do not visit during scheduled activities that he enjoys. He may look forward to the activities all week and feel disappointed if he cannot attend. Also, do not visit when he prefers to rest.

Inquire when your loved one is scheduled for specific types of care so that you can observe how they are carried out. For example, occasionally be present when he is scheduled to receive medication so that you make sure he receives it in a timely way. Sometimes visit at bath time, to ensure it is done unhurriedly and with compassion. Occasionally request a guest tray and eat with him so that you can observe whether special dietary restrictions are followed and whether he receives the mealtime assistance that he needs. On Sunday, arrive early and sit in his room to make sure that if he has been promised a ride to the chapel service, it happens.

Keep a journal or log of your visits. Notes help you to be more aware of changes in your loved one's condition. They also are a record to which you can refer if you begin to experience problems with her care. While it may seem tedious to keep a journal, you will probably find it useful. Hopefully, instead of needing it for documentation of problems, you will peruse it and thank God for the good care your loved one receives and the extended time you have together because of that care. Be sure to include heartwarming, positive experiences that you will want to remember and cherish.

Communication. See chapter 5 for specific communication tips and topics for conversation. Relate to your loved one as you related to her prior to the move. Tell her what is going on in your family, your life, and the world. Inquire about how she is experiencing life in her new home. Ask her for advice, because everyone craves to be needed. When possible, vary the format of your visits: take her for a walk, a ride in a wheelchair, a ride in your car, or out to eat in a restaurant.

Bring a small gift as a memento of your time together. For example, your loved one may enjoy homemade cookies made from a favorite family recipe, a new family photograph, a church bulletin, fresh flowers (perhaps from your garden), a new item of clothing, stamps, lemon drops, a new CD of her favorite music, a large-print crossword puzzle book, a Sudoku book, a homemade picture drawn and colored by a grandchild, yarn for knitting, a devotional book, a magazine, or a copy of the local newspaper.

Allow your loved one to have a bad day. If she is out of sorts, encourage her to talk about how she feels and what is causing her feelings. Accept her feelings. Take complaints that she has about the care facility seriously and investigate them—even if the complaints seem ridiculous. They might be true, and you might be the only person she feels that she can tell without suffering retaliation. You also might be the only person who believes her. Follow the tips for correcting problems found at the end of this chapter.

If your loved one becomes difficult to visit due to behavior problems, you may need to modify how you visit. For example, if she makes hurtful statements to you and always complains about you, visit less frequently or for shorter periods of time. Try not to argue. If your loved one has always been critical and angry, do not expect her personality to improve now. Taking care of yourself is part of your spiritual calling. While she has professionals caring for her 24/7, you may not have anyone other than you and God taking care of you. Engage in personal spiritual and psychological self-care.

Observations. When you visit in your loved one's room, make strategic observations. Is water readily available? Does he know where the fresh water is placed and when it is supposed to be changed? Can he reach the water container and hold it? Does he remember to drink? If your loved one is prone to dehydration, ask the staff to give him a drink every time they enter the room. Such a small request will not take much time from their busy schedules.

If your loved one has been assessed to be incontinent, observe whether this evaluation was made because his call light was not answered in a timely manner and he was unable to reach the bathroom in time to avoid an accident.

Also observe whether he has difficulty sitting or lying in bed. Is he restless? Is he in pain? If he frequently tries to readjust his position, he may have pressure sores and may need special padding placed in his wheelchair and bed, and he may need to be moved or turned every two hours. Do all you can to prevent pressure sores, because they are difficult to cure, as well as painful.

When you visit during mealtime, observe whether he is eating well. If the staff comments to you that he does not like to eat, be a detective. Is the food seasoned the way he prefers so that it tastes good? Is he served food entrees that he likes? If not, he may choose not to eat. Are the other residents at his table doing anything to prevent him from eating, such as placing food they don't want on his plate, removing food from his plate and eating it, refusing to pass condiments to him, drooling, consistently coughing, etc.? A change of table assignment might make the dining experience more pleasant and amenable to good nutrition. If necessary, request that special food items be prepared for him. While nutritional supplements may carry an extra monetary charge, the added expense may be essential for good health.

PSYCHOLOGICAL STRESS FOR CAREGIVERS OF RESIDENTS

Caregivers whose loved ones relocate to a care facility may periodically experience a "dark night of the soul" as they think about the reasons that necessitated the move and about how their lives and their loved ones' lives have changed. Even though it is a relief for caregivers to know their loved ones are receiving comprehensive round-the-clock care, the psychological adjustment can be as great for them as for their care recipients. It is common for caregivers to struggle with the following feelings:

Guilt. If you play the "should have" game with yourself, don't. You may feel guilty because you believe that you should have done more to avoid relocation. But you probably did more than many people do—otherwise, you would not feel so bad. This is especially true if your newly admitted loved one begs you to take her home with you. This situation is filled with angst. You may think: "If I was a devoted caregiver, I wouldn't have abandoned her to the care of strangers. Instead, I should have quit my job and provided total care for her at home, even if I was almost completely exhausted. I could have taken out a second mortgage to hire live-in help to take care of her."

Deal with guilt feelings by reminding yourself that not only did you and your loved one pray about the relocation decision but you also evaluated all the facts and mutually agreed that she needed more care than what you can provide, obtain, or afford at home. Because you made your decision prayerfully and seriously, bless your decision rather than second-guessing it. If the relocation decision was made against your loved one's wishes, it was a heartbreaking process. But because you did what you had to do, again, bless your decision.

After your loved one has been a resident for a while, other sources of guilt may develop. For example, perhaps her roommate yells during the night or is abusive—and you never anticipated such dynamics. Rather than putting up with the roommate's behavior, formally request a different room assignment, as well as request that the staff regularly monitor the situation until the room change occurs. Another example: Perhaps your loved one's clothing is lost or damaged, and you feel guilty that you are not doing her laundry. Double-check that her name is affixed to each item of clothing and that the fabric of her clothing is easy to launder. If you have done this, lodge a formal complaint. Don't feel guilty for complaining. These are legitimate concerns that need to be corrected. Bless your decision to speak up. Do not be timid. If you do not advocate for your loved one, who will?

Fear. It is normal to be afraid. You may be afraid that your loved one (or you) will not adjust well to the new situation, that friends or neighbors will criticize you for placing your loved one in a care facility, that he will not receive timely help to go to the bathroom and will have an embarrassing accident, that the staff will not give him enough time to finish meals because he needs to eat slowly in order to chew and digest his food, and that the staff will forget to call you if he has an emergency. Share your fears with the staff so that possible problems can be addressed before they occur. Thank the staff when they respond compassionately and effectively to you and your loved one.

Depression. There are many situations that may contribute to your depression, some as a result of your loved one's move to a care facility and some because of her declining health. Your loved one's move may have reduced her life to one room, a few treasured possessions, and a bulletin board. She may be unable to leave her room because she is on a medication that makes it necessary for her to remain close to the bathroom. Your loved one may have developed a tendency to cry due to changes in her life. She may need to use a walker or wheelchair for the first time and, later, possibly change from a wheelchair to a geriatric chair because her body is weak and needs more support. Her inability to eat regular food and need for pureed food and thickened water is another sad sign of her declining health. Her behavioral changes caused by dementia, such as belligerence and hitting, may be completely opposite to her past life behavior. Her inability to remember who you are may be the saddest change of all. Yes, sad changes are occurring for both you and your care recipient. Give yourself permission to feel your depression and find safe ways to express your feelings.

This book gives you many guidelines for caring for yourself when you go through the relocation of your loved one to a supervised facility. These include following the spiritual and psychological nurturing tips in chapters 3 and 4, reading the Scripture passages and praying the prayers at the end of each chapter, referring to appendix E for additional Bible passages, and referring to appendix F for caregiving Web sites. Remember that God cares for you.

RELATING TO STAFF

Thanks and praise go a long way in making the care facility staff feel valued and appreciated. Often they are so overworked and criticized by families, one another, the administration, residents, and visitors that they hunger for a kind word. When a staff member provides good care to your loved one and to you, send a short written note of appreciation to her or him, to the staff person's supervisor, and to the administrator. Request that the compliment be placed in the worker's personnel file and included at the next performance review. In the note, ask the staff person to continue the good work.

At Christmas, provide a large box of candy or fruit basket for your loved one's nursing unit, along with a note of thanks. At Easter, bring an Easter lily to the nurses' station with a card to thank the staff for their high-quality care and compassionate service. At Thanksgiving, send your loved one's nursing station a thank-you card and request that it be posted for all those who take care of him to read.

Help the staff learn to know your loved one as a person and not just a case. Bring a collage of photographs that picture him in different roles in life. Include family photos, pictures of your loved one's home and pets, pictures of special times and achievements, and pictures of his church and favorite vacation spot. Post the collage in a noticeable location. Bring wall hangings of his handcrafted items or certificates of appreciation that he received in past years. Thank the staff for taking the time to get to know your loved one as he was when he was younger.

Role model for the staff how you want your loved one to be treated. Extend compassion and kindness to him in front of them. Ask the staff to give him encouragement and TLC (tender loving care) when you are absent, because he is very dear to you and to God. Tell them that you always try to touch his heart and spirit so that he will know he is loved and important. Ask the staff to do the same. Sometimes the most compassionate and unhurried persons are the housekeepers and maintenance workers.

When you converse with the staff, model the Golden Rule. (Do unto others as you would have them do unto you.) Frequently in health care facilities, the way in which those in authority treat the staff is also the way the staff treats the residents. Treat them well. Be Christlike toward them. Hopefully they will be Christlike toward your loved one. Let them know that God loves them and so do you.

HOW TO MAKE A COMPLAINT

If you have questions about the rights of your loved one in the care facility, request a copy of the "Resident's Rights" document that should have been given to your loved one upon admission. Know your rights!

When you want to make a request or complaint, the following options are available.

Approach the staff person directly. Approach the staff person who is directly involved in the problem. It is also helpful if you communicate with the worker's supervisor. Put the complaint in writing, because your documentation later can be used as proof that you contacted the staff. Include as many details as possible, such as the time the incident occurred, names of staff people involved, others who witnessed the incident, and ill effects it caused your loved one and you.

Attend your loved one's care conferences. Upon admission inquire when the first care conference will be held and how frequently follow-up conferences will occur. If you are employed, try diligently to schedule time off so that you can attend. If attendance is impossible, request that both your employer and your loved one's care facility make it possible for you to attend via speakerphone.

The purposes of care conferences are:

- to inform you and your loved one about her medical, pharmaceutical, nutritional, rehabilitative, psychological, socialization, spiritual, and future needs;
- to answer your and your loved one's questions;
- to respond to your and your loved one's requests.

Be assertive. Do not just sit back and listen. Ask questions and make requests for high-quality care. Perhaps you want your loved one to be examined by a physician, to have a pharmaceutical review to make sure she is not being over- or under-medicated, to receive a nutritional supplement, to receive physical therapy to strengthen her legs so she can ambulate better, to attend group activities for higher functioning residents in order to provide appropriate intellectual stimulation and interaction, to see a psychologist and be treated for depression, to be addressed by name by the staff, or to be given assistance to attend chapel worship services. Remember that you and your loved one are paying the bill. You have the right to good care. If you need to install a video camera on a wall in your loved one's room to directly observe the care she receives, do so.

Following the care conference, allow adequate time for the staff to implement the agreed-upon requests. When you think enough time has passed, inquire of both your loved one and the staff whether your requests have been carried out. Keep in mind that if your loved one is forgetful, she may not accurately remember if something has occurred. If no positive action has been taken, speak up!

Encourage your care recipient to attend Resident Council meetings. Find out when the Resident Council meets, who leads it, and if the residents are given transportation assistance to attend the meeting. Encourage your loved one to attend and to speak up. These monthly meetings are optimally led by residents (with one staff person's assistance) and are for the benefit of the residents. If, however, only a few residents attend, strive to find out why the attendance is poor. Perhaps the residents do not think they are taken seriously. Perhaps the great majority of the residents are cognitively low functioning. Perhaps the residents believe that if a staff person leads the meeting the outcome is decided by the administration before the meeting takes place.

Ideally, the Resident Council empowers the residents to know that their voices are heard as individuals and as a group. For example, if residents enjoyed a special menu for a meal, they can request that it be served again; if lukewarm coffee is delivered to their tables, they can request that it be served hotter; if laundry items are not returned to their rooms, they can report them missing and request that an investigation be held to find the lost items; if call lights are not answered in a timely manner, they can request that the lights be answered promptly; if they cannot sleep at night because the staff talks loudly outside their doors, they can request that the staff go elsewhere to visit; if they want to have a program about a specific topic of interest, they can request help in obtaining one; if they smell or see mold, they can request that it be eliminated.

All compliments, requests, and complaints made by the residents during the meeting must be taken seriously by the facility and responded to in the most timely and positive manner possible. In a nursing home, state and federal examiners evaluate the facility's response to the residents' requests during the facility's annual evaluative survey. Thus resident participation in the meetings is important for the betterment of life in the home.

Attend Family Council meetings. Family Council meetings are a venue for you to share your thoughts about the facility with other family caregivers, to effect positive change, and to share your feelings with and receive support from persons in similar caregiving situations. If there is no Family Council, find out why. You may need to talk with other family caregivers and together request that the facility begin a Family Council.

Some Family Councils invite a different staff person to attend each meeting and make a short presentation about her or his department so that you can learn more both about that discipline and about the staff person. The more questions you ask, the more you learn. The more you advocate for yourself and your loved one, the more positive your experience will be in the care facility.

Talk with the facility administrator. If you try unsuccessfully to effect positive change for your loved one through the above channels, make an appointment with the administrator to discuss the situation. Bring all your facts and documentation to the meeting. You also may want to bring another person with you to witness the meeting. As you try to resolve the problem, remember that if the administrator responds unsatisfactorily, you have further recourse (see next paragraph). Do not allow the administrator to focus all the blame for the situation upon you or your loved one. Keep in mind the Resident's Bill of Rights that is posted at the care facility. You deserve respect and serious consideration for the problem you present.

Contact your ombudsperson, OSHA (Occupational Safety and Health Administration), or the State Board of Health. If you have tried to effect a positive and necessary change for your loved one (especially of a critical nature) through all other possible channels of communication (including talking with the administrator), but have been unsuccessful, look on the walls near the main office or in the foyer for a poster stating how to lodge a formal complaint. If you want to ask someone to intercede on your behalf, contact the ombudsperson for your area. Keep in mind, however, some ombudspersons have close, positive ties to the facility. If you question the safety and health of the building, contact OSHA. If you believe your loved one is receiving inadequate or incompetent care that is detrimental to her overall health, contact your State Department of Health.

Your loved one deserves to be treated with honor, dignity, and competence. This is what God wants for all his people. While it takes courage to lodge a formal complaint, take heart. God will give you the guidance and strength to do so.

DISCHARGE PLANNING

If your loved one is medically capable of being discharged from the care facility and you decide to bring him home, obtain the discharge date as soon as possible—because you will need time to make preparations. Ask the discharge planner what equipment (see chapter 6) your loved one will need. Locate, hire, and schedule home health care to help you, especially immediately upon his return home. Obtain prescriptions for medications and fill them in advance of the discharge. Do not eliminate any medications. Ask the discharge planner or social worker about home care insurance benefits or government financial assistance. If you have not been given home-going instructions by the medical staff, request that the discharge planner obtain written instructions for you.

A word of caution: It is not a good idea to allow your loved one to leave the facility against medical advice, even if you become exasperated with poor-quality care. Doing so can have serious ramifications, such as not receiving insurance coverage for home health care, not being given prescriptions for medications, not knowing how to carry out the medical procedures that were done in the facility, and not being allowed readmission if the need arises.

If he leaves AMA (against medical advice), you might quickly discover that you are unable to adequately take care of him and need an immediate admission to another facility. Quick admissions are difficult to accomplish, especially during evening, nighttime, and weekend hours. It is better for your loved one to remain in the facility—even one with which you might be displeased—while you look for a different facility, rather than compromise his medical condition due to a lack of patience.

TAKE HEART

Care facilities can provide a wonderful, loving, and competent home for your loved one. Church-related homes and Eden Alternative homes offer holistic care (body, mind, and spirit) to their clients as well as provide spiritual care for you. I recommend these homes as a great option for your loved one and you.

Residents of care facilities, like all of us, have been created in God's image and proclaimed to be "very good." One day you also may live in a supervised home. Visit your loved one in a care facility with the same kindness, love, and regularity with which you in that situation would want to be visited. Take heart. God will give you the guidance and strength to do so. You will never regret being an attentive and loving family caregiver to your loved one who lives in a care facility.

SCRIPTURE

"Love is patient, love is kind. It does not envy, it does not boast, it is not proud. It is not rude, it is not self-seeking, it is not easily angered, it keeps no record of wrongs. Love does not delight in evil but rejoices with the truth. It always protects, always trusts, always hopes, always perseveres" (1 Corinthians 13:4–7).

PRAYER FOR CAREGIVERS

Dear God, we made the decision for my loved one to move into a care facility. It wasn't easy, but we did it. We made our decision seriously, prayerfully, and factually. Help us to bless our decision rather than second-guess it. I thank you for the professional caregivers in her (his) new home. Fill them with your Spirit so that they respond to my loved one competently and compassionately. Bless my loved one as she (he) adjusts to the new home. Love, support, and befriend her (him). Help me to reach out to my loved one with empathy, patience, kindness, love, and peace. Keep ever before me my threefold spiritual calling to love you, to love my neighbor (my loved one, the staff, and the other residents), and to love myself. Fill me with your peace today and every day. I need you. In Jesus' name I pray. Amen.

Chapter Twelve
Dealing With Your Loved One's Dying and Death Process

The death of your care recipient may be the most poignant event in your life. Even if you have experienced other deaths—such as the death of a friend, relative, or colleague—your loved one's death can be more profound because you have invested a great deal of time and energy into deeply loving and caring for him in the last phase of his life.

God said to Moses in the Old Testament, "Take off your sandals, for the place where you are standing is holy ground" (Exodus 3:5). Being with your loved one as he is dying, and (if possible) being with him at the actual time of death, is a blessing and honor. Other than your own death, it could be the holiest experience you will ever have.

As the sacred moment of death draws near, your spiritual caregiving calling takes on its deepest dimension. Consider the following caregiving goals as your loved one is dying:

- I will help my loved one draw close to Jesus so that he will die in spiritual peace.

- I will keep him as comfortable as possible as the end draws near.

- I will relate to him in such a way that after his death, I will be at peace because I cared for him with a Christlike love.

Knowing that you are doing everything you can for your loved one, that Jesus' promise of salvation is for all who believe in him, and that God promises to comfort and strengthen you after your loved one's death will help you not to lose heart at this most sacred time.

ANTICIPATING DEATH

When you initially realize that your loved one is nearing the time of death, it may be a traumatic time for you. This realization may come upon you unexpectedly as you perform a routine caregiving task or as your loved one develops a medical problem. For example, when you check on her when she is sleeping and you do not immediately see her chest move up and down, you may fear that her heart has stopped. Or if your loved one contracts bronchitis, you may fear that it will turn into pneumonia and she will die. As these and other similar experiences lead you to accept the fact that your loved one will eventually die, the inevitability of her death may remain on your mind. Anticipatory thoughts of death are common for caregivers, and they frequently result in distressful feelings.

In order to assist your loved one to pragmatically prepare for death (whether or not death is imminent), encourage her to complete two documents that will make the end time easier and more peaceful for both of you.

First, encourage her to complete a *health care directive.* Contact a local hospital, medical clinic, or law attorney for the elderly to obtain a copy of the health care directive that is legally effective in your state, or turn to appendix F for a Web site that provides information about health care directives for all states. Encourage your loved one to complete her health care directive as soon as possible.

If your loved one is reluctant to complete this form—perhaps because she has trouble facing the inevitability of death—try approaching her in the following way: "Do you remember when your neighbor was seriously ill and how difficult it was for her adult children when she was dying? They didn't know what her preferences for medical care were. Have you thought about your medical wishes if you are faced with a time when you cannot think, reason, or speak for yourself? This, unfortunately, could happen due to a serious accident, terminal illness, advanced state of dementia, stroke, or the normal aging process. When that time comes for you, I want to honor you by following your wishes rather than trying to guess what they might be. I have completed my health care directive and hope that you will do the same. I'll help you write it if you would like me to do so. Or if you'd rather have someone else help you with it that would be fine too. Would you do this for me?"

Your loved one needs to be as specific as possible in her health care directive. For example: If she is in a critical medical condition and incapable of making medical decisions, does she want to receive nutrition and hydration if the prognosis indicates little or no positive recovery? Does she want CPR (cardiopulmonary resuscitation) used, even if she will be in a compromised medical condition if she survives? Does she want pain medications, even if they make her unresponsive or hasten her death? Whom does she want to be her health care agent and articulate her medical wishes if she is unable to do so?

After your care recipient has prepared her health care directive, including naming her health care agent, it must be communicated with her medical doctor and copies placed in her chart and at her preferred hospital. Distribute copies to all appropriate family members as well. If her wishes are not communicated, there is no point in preparing such a document.

Second, encourage your care recipient to complete the *Preplanning Your Funeral or Memorial Service Form* (see appendix B) as soon as possible, preferably in advance of a serious medical situation. If your loved one would like help in completing the funeral form, you may help her or she may contact her pastor or mortician. After she completes the form, she will be glad she did; and you, the caregiver, will be relieved to know her preferences for hymns, Scripture readings, special music, a specific theme, pallbearers, and other details so that you can honor her wishes. Place the completed form in an accessible location. Do not place it in a bank safe-deposit box, because you cannot access it during evenings or weekends. Plus, if your name is not also on her safe-deposit box, it can take weeks (in some cases) to open the box.

As you and your loved one select a funeral home, talk to several morticians and compare prices. A federal law known as the Funeral Rule has been passed for your protection. Funeral homes are required to give you free copies of their price lists, in person or over the telephone. If a mortuary refuses to do so, find a different one.

There is something else you personally can do as you anticipate your loved one's death. Write a letter of gratitude to her. In your letter, share your heartfelt love, thoughts, and feelings. Describe what your loved one means to you now and what she has meant to you in the past. Assure her of your never-ending love. Describe how your love for her has deepened over the course of time. Thank her for all she has shared with you, such as lessons in life, Christian values, a sense of humor, fun times, hobbies, skills, role modeling, sacrifices, love, comfort, support, and opportunities. Assure your loved one that God loves her.

After you have written your letter of gratitude, read it aloud to her, and give it to her so that she can periodically reread it for comfort and assurance. Keep a copy for yourself. Again, the sooner you do this the better, so that she has ample time to cherish it before she dies. Remember, you are living out your final spiritual caregiving calling with your loved one in the sacred closing time of her earthly life.

HOSPICE

Hospice organizations provide high-quality, compassionate care for both you and your loved one. Hospice helps when an individual has either been given a prognosis of less than six months to live or has chosen not to seek curative treatment for a terminal condition. Hospice care is available in private homes, apartments, convalescent hospitals, nursing homes, and hospice centers. Approximately 855,000 Americans utilized hospice services in 2003.[1] Medicare frequently pays for hospice services for senior citizens.

The goals of hospice are to keep your loved one as physically comfortable as possible, to provide emotional and spiritual support, and to help make the dying, death, and bereavement experience as meaningful as possible. In the process, hospice workers relate to both of you with dignity and respect, as well as invite you, the caregiver, to participate as fully as you wish in caring for your loved one. Because of hospice services, feelings of loneliness that you and your loved one experience near the end of his life can be partially alleviated.

The hospice team includes many of the following medical disciplines: nurses, dietitians, chaplains, physical therapists, speech therapists, music therapists, occupational therapists, social workers, home health care workers, and trained volunteers. While hospice physicians are experts in alleviating physical pain, they advocate neither hastening nor postponing death. They advise you and your loved one about the side effects of prescription pain medications and honestly inform you if a medication causes sleepiness or unresponsiveness or hastens death. Trained hospice volunteers are available to sit and tenderly visit with you and your loved one, run errands, and provide respite care.

The hospice team meets regularly both as a staff and with you. They update you about your loved one's evolving care plan, educate you about the dying process so that you know what to expect, offer you support, and are often available 24/7.

Contact your local hospital for the names and addresses of hospice organizations in your area. The earlier you and your loved one are served by hospice, the more meaningful the dying process will be and the more support both of you will receive. Too many families wait until their loved one's last few days before utilizing hospice services.

FEELINGS OF CAREGIVERS

No matter how much you try to emotionally prepare for the time of your care recipient's death, you may never be fully prepared. The loss may be too profound and painful for you to be totally prepared. For example, your loved one's death may mean the loss of a cherished long-term relationship. If it is your parent who dies, it means that you lose the one whose voice you first heard, whose face you first saw, and whose heart taught you how to be a loving person. While your loved one's death will create an emptiness for you, try not to lose heart. Your loved one will live on in everything you do as you incorporate his positive values and lessons into your life.

Be kind to yourself as your loved one is dying. Allow yourself to feel your feelings. Share them with a trusted friend, relative, or professional, and with God in prayer. Do not fall into the common trap of focusing so intently upon the one who is dying that you neglect *your* feelings and needs. Refer to chapters 3 and 4 for spiritual and psychological self-care tips.

Common feelings experienced by caregivers whose loved ones are dying include:

- **Gratitude to God** because of the love, life, and gifts your loved one shared with you throughout his life. You also may be grateful that you are able to lovingly share of yourself with him.

- **Depression** because, in spite of all your caregiving efforts, you cannot prevent your loved one's deterioration and inevitable death. Emotional numbness, insomnia, and tears may be symptoms of your depression.

- **Anger** because your loved one who enjoyed being in control of his life is now vulnerable and dependent upon caregivers. If your loved one is suffering during his last days, his suffering may not seem fair because not everyone who dies suffers. You also may be angry if the cause of his pending death (such as cancer, stroke, or accident) has no cure.

- **Fear** that you will lose control if you express your feelings, that you will make a wrong medical decision, that the medical staff will bring you bad news, that your loved one will die when you are absent from the room, that your loved one has not made peace with God and is not ready to die, or that you will be unable to get along without your loved one after he dies.

- **Hope** because your loved one knows Jesus, whose promise of eternal life is for all who believe in him.

Remember two things about your feelings. First, all previous losses in your life—whether they are the loss of relationship, employment, home, identity, self-esteem—compound the intensity of your feelings as you anticipate the death of your loved one. Second, God will not abandon you.

FEELINGS OF DYING PERSONS

People who are dying approach death in a variety of ways. Some persons accept a terminal diagnosis, while others never accept it as a reality. Some persons remain engaged in life, while others lose interest and give up. Some individuals enjoy conversation, while others do not want to talk, perhaps because talking takes too much physical or emotional energy. Some persons fear death and try to stay awake because they worry that if they fall asleep they will die, while others prefer to sleep because they are at peace and long to join God in eternity.

In the years, months, weeks, and days leading up to death, your loved one may experience feelings of loss and grief resulting from:

- social death of relationships as she has less and less contact with friends and family, and as she realizes that one day she will be remembered in memories and pictures only;

- psychological death of her personality as she withdraws from people around her or as she experiences cognitive loss;

- existential death of her unfulfilled goals;

- biological death of her diminishing appearance, performance, physical health, and consciousness.

Help your loved one to experience spiritual peace as she approaches her end time. Share Bible verses that focus upon God's promise of eternal life through faith in Jesus Christ. A list of Scripture passages is included later in this chapter. Remind her, "God so loved the world that he gave his one and only Son, that whoever believes in him shall not perish but have eternal life" (John 3:16). If, however, she has been somewhat distant from God throughout her life and has concerns about meeting God due to a fear of retribution for sins, also share John 3:17 with her: "God did not send his Son into the world to condemn the world, but to save the world through him." You may also want to share 1 John 1:9: "If we confess our sins, he is faithful and just and will forgive us our sins and purify us from all unrighteousness." Be God's vehicle of peace for her. Assist her to make each remaining day a sacred moment as she draws closer to God and God draws closer to her.

COMFORT CARES

Make your loved one's last days as physically comfortable as possible. Never neglect caring for him during this holy time. If he is in pain, speak with his physician about pain medication. Refer to your records to know what medications have effectively alleviated his pain in the past. Ask the physician whether a specific pain medication will increase your loved one's sleepiness or induce an unresponsive state. If the medication has these side effects, unless your loved one experiences unbearable pain and requests the medication, you may want to delay using it so that you, other family members, and (possibly) friends have the opportunity to say good-bye to him while he is still aware of his surroundings. Allow him to be in control of his dying process as much as possible.

The following physical cares may make your loved one more comfortable:

- If he is able to get out of bed, have him occasionally sit in a comfortable chair or on the side of the bed. This alleviates stiffness, pain, bedsores, and skin breakdown. Change his position every two hours, whenever possible. Whether he sits or reclines, inquire whether he wants to wear street clothes or sleepwear.

- If he is bedridden, use a soft pillow under his arms or legs, behind his back when he lies on his side, or between his knees to prevent a skin breakdown. Smooth the sheet under his body so there are no uncomfortable wrinkles. Add a soft blanket or remove a blanket, as needed. Pad the sides of the hospital bed with pillows.

- If he has a breathing problem, take him outside (if possible) or ventilate the room by opening a window or using a fan. Try not to create a draft. If he is uncomfortably warm, place a cool, moist cloth on his forehead. Unless he has an allergy, use scented candles, potpourri, or aromatherapy to rid the room of the smell of death, if there is one.

- Adjust the lighting level in the room to match your loved one's usual preferences. A soft light may be most appropriate. Use eye drops to prevent dry, itchy, or painful eyes or blurred vision.

- Wash and gently comb or brush her hair. If she usually wears makeup, ask her if she wants to do so now. Ask him if he wants to be shaved, or (if he is always clean-shaven) shave him.

- Care for his mouth by regularly placing Vaseline on his lips, having him rinse his mouth (if he can), swabbing his mouth to moisten it, providing sugarless candy (if he will not choke on it), offering him crushed ice (with the permission of the medical staff if he is in an institution), giving room-temperature water (if he doesn't like ice), or giving him a Popsicle or wet washcloth to suck on. Ask if he wants to continue wearing his dentures or partials. While some people are more comfortable without dentures, others want to wear them.

- If appropriate, use a straw to give him fluids by lowering it into a beverage glass, placing your finger over the outside end as you remove the straw, and slowly releasing the water into his mouth. Feed him according to his wishes and ability to eat.

- Gently rub his face and massage his limbs and back with oil or lotion. If he trembles, gently place your hand on the area as calming comfort.

PHYSICAL SIGNS THAT DEATH IS NEAR

Because the following physical signs sometimes occur when death is imminent, do not be surprised or confused if you observe them in your loved one. Ask your loved one's physician or nurse about other signs you observe. By all means do not chastise your loved one when some of these symptoms appear.

Sleepiness or lapses in and out of consciousness and responsiveness. As death draws near, your loved one may sleep and be more difficult to arouse. Even though she may not respond when you speak to her, she will (in all likelihood) hear you, unless she is hard of hearing and not wearing her hearing aid. Identify yourself so that you do not make her wonder who you are. If she becomes confused about your identity, the confusion might be caused by the deterioration of her medical condition, changes in vision, medications, or tiredness.

Changes in breathing. Your loved one's breathing may become inaudible or uneven, with extended pauses between breaths. If she gasps for air, she is not necessarily uncomfortable. Elevate her head to help her breathe better or add a small rotating fan to the room to move the air, as long as it does not blow a cold draft on her. A cooler room promotes better breathing than a hot room, although you do not want your loved one to be uncomfortably cold. Loosen the clothing around her neck and make sure the clothing is not heavy. Ask the medical staff to give her supplemental oxygen through a nosepiece or face mask. A rattling sound (caused by oral secretions collecting in the throat) can be more distracting to you than to her. Try turning her on her side to promote quieter breathing. Ask the medical staff if it is appropriate to use suction to remove secretions. Her last breaths may sound like sighs spaced apart with long pauses between them.

Seeing visions, reaching, and talking. Some dying persons see relatives who have previously died—and talk to them. Some people also see Jesus, God, angels, a tunnel, a bright light, a review of their lives, a heavenly green meadow, or the peace of heaven. Some may reach out to loved ones in heaven or to Jesus, whom they see coming for them. Do not dispute what your loved one tells you. Instead, ask, "Who do you see?" "What do you see?" "What do you need?" Be kind and loving. You are sharing a very sacred time.

Physical signs. Your loved one may exhibit some of the following physical signs: lowered blood pressure and heart rate, unpredictable muscle contractions, decreased ability to swallow, grimacing or clenching teeth, restlessness, pulling or picking at the sheets, trying to remove clothing, loss of urine or bowel control, or inability to move. These are normal signs that the end is near.

COMMUNICATION NEAR THE END OF LIFE

When your loved one is near death, honor her with your love, tenderness, dignity, respect, and compassion. Remember what a sacred journey both of you are on. It is the holy ground of your care recipient's last days on this earth.

Assure her of your presence by placing your face in front of her face so she can see you. Have a loving expression on your face. Hold her hand, sit near her, gently stroke her, and give her a tender hug.

Do not insist upon constant conversation and do not talk over or around your loved one, engaging in idle chatter with someone else in the room. Ignoring her in this way can lead her to think she is incapable of talking about something of significance with you as well as make her feel isolated, lonely, and abandoned, even at the hour of death. Give your dying loved one your attention. Soon you will not be able to give her your attention. After her death, you can engage in conversation with relatives and friends. Sitting quietly is biblical. Remember what the psalmist wrote: "Be still, and know that I am God" (Psalm 46:10). Your loved one needs to rest. She is nearing eternity. Give her peace. Pray with her and for her.

Do not talk or whisper with others outside your loved one's door. This should be common sense, but people unfortunately frequently do it without thinking. Your loved one may become alarmed and think that you and others know more about her condition than she does. She also may misunderstand what she overhears. Do not raise her anxiety in this way; instead, let her focus her thoughts upon meeting God face-to-face.

The deathbed (and area outside your loved one's room) is no place to bring up family conflict or conflict about medical decisions. Your loved one needs peace and tranquility. If you feel compelled to have such conversations, do so at another time and in a different place. Your primary focus at this time should be your threefold spiritual calling: to love God, to love your care recipient, and to love yourself. Don't fall into the abyss of argumentation.

The following tips may be helpful as you talk with your loved one who is dying:

- Do not avoid talking about the topic of death and his feelings about dying. Use some of the conversation topics related to death and dying included in appendix D (Spiritual Journey Exercise). Accept his feelings about death rather than contradicting or interrupting them. Say, "Tell me more." Repeat back to him brief acknowledgments that you hear and understand what he is telling you.

- If you are unsure how to respond to your loved one who denies his terminal condition and asks, "I'm getting better, aren't I?" you may want to respond, "What has the doctor told you?"

- When your loved one reminisces, help him to see God's preshis terminal condition and asks, "I'm getting better, aren't I?" you may want to respond, "What has the doctor told you?"

- When your loved one reminisces, help him to see God's presence in his experiences. Thank him for sharing his thoughts. If he begins to cry, allow him to do so.

- Focus upon him. Ask, "How are you feeling?" "Do you feel like talking?" "How can I help you?" Do not talk about people who have gone through similar situations. Your loved one's situation is unique.

- If your loved one lashes out in anger, he may misdirect his anger toward you or the medical staff, while in reality, he is angry at his disease, illness, or circumstance. Allow him to be angry. Do not take it personally. You may be the only person with whom he dares express anger. Tell him, "It's okay to be angry." Read to him Psalms 58 and 109 if he is angry at people, and Psalms 22, 44:23–24, and 60 if he is angry with God. At the same time, if you are angry, do not make your loved one the target of your anger. Find someone else who will listen to you.

- If he is depressed, assure him that you are doing everything possible to make him feel better, that you will continue to do so, and that you are with him.

- Ask him if he has any unfinished business that you or someone else can help him complete. Help him to leave this world feeling that everything is finished and resolved.

- Assure him of God's love and the gift of salvation for all who believe. Use a calm, gentle voice when reading Scripture, offering prayers, and talking with him. Remember that your words may be the last words he hears. Think through them carefully. It is a profound honor and privilege to offer these words as your last gift to him. Know that as you comfort your loved one, God is present with both of you: "For where two or three come together in my name, there am I with them" (Matthew 18:20).

Read the following Scripture passages to comfort your loved one as well as support you during his dying process:

- Psalm 17:15; 23; 25:1–6; 27:1–5, 13–14; 31:5; 42; 43; 46; 91; 103; 116; 121; 130; 146:1–9

- Ecclesiastes 3:1–8

- Isaiah 41:10; 43:1–5a; 49:15–16; 54:10

- Lamentations 3:22–26

- Matthew 8:23–27; 11:28–30; 25:34; 28:1–10

- Mark 16:1–6

- Luke 2:29–32; 22:14, 19–20; 23:42–43; 24:1–12

- John 3:16–17; 5:24–29; 6:45–51; 10:27–28; 11:25; 13:34–35; 14:1–6; 15:1, 4–5, 7–11

- Romans 6:3–9; 8:38–39; 14:7–8

- 2 Corinthians 4:13–18

- Ephesians 2:8

- Philippians 1:9–26; 4:4–9

- Colossians 3:12–17

- 1 Thessalonians 4:13–18; 5:17

- 2 Timothy 4:7–8

- 1 Peter 1:3–9

- 1 John 2:25; 3:16; 4:7–12, 16–18; 5:11, 13, 20

- Titus 3:4–7

- Jude 21

- Revelation 7:9–17; 21:1–7; 21:22–22:6

If your loved one is a member or friend of an area congregation, inform the pastor that your loved one is dying and request visits. Even when a facility chaplain is available, your loved one's pastor will appreciate the notification and your loved one will be pleased when the pastor comes.

SAYING GOOD-BYE

If you are a person who does not readily share your thoughts and feelings with others, you still need to say good-bye to your loved one—for her sake, so that she leaves this world assured about your love for her, and for your sake, so that you have no regrets for failing to do so.

What do you say? If you already wrote a letter of gratitude and shared it with your loved one, repeat some of your thoughts from that letter and add other heartfelt thoughts and feelings. For example:

- Say, "I love you" many times.

- Tell her how important she has been in your life. Assure her that she will always be important to you and that you will always try to honor her memory by following in her loving footsteps.

- Thank her for everything she did for you and enumerate the most important things.

- Affirm her for being a courageous and loving (and other attributes that apply to her) spouse, parent, grandparent, or friend.

- Give her permission to die. Tell her: "It's okay to let go. Be at peace."

If you say good-bye to your loved one based upon the visible signs of death, and your loved one does not die, you will need to say good-bye to her again, at another time. Do not neglect doing so just because you said good-bye previously. She will again need and cherish your words of love and assurance.

THE TIME OF DEATH

The time of your loved one's death is the most sacred time you, as caregiver, will experience (other than your own death). Theologian Henri Nouwen stated, "Death does not have the last word. We can look at [our dying loved ones] . . . and give them hope; we can hold their bodies in our arms. And we can trust that mightier arms than ours will receive them and give them the peace and joy they deserve."[2]

The following "Time of Death Service" will help both you and your dying loved one to let go and let God be with you at the sacred moment of death. As you share this ritual, feel free to modify, paraphrase, and adapt it (including its length) to your personal situation. You may want to do different parts of it at different times in your loved one's dying process rather than all at once.

Time of Death Service

We begin in the name of the Father, Son, and Holy Spirit.

_____, you have been very important to me throughout my entire life. I remember especially . . . (for example) that you gave me the gift of faith by taking me to church and Sunday school, that you are my role model of faith, that you gave me the opportunity to take part in extracurricular school activities, etc.

Thank you for the lessons of life you taught me. They will remain with me forever—lessons such as . . . (for example) the importance of facing the struggles of life with courage, the importance of turning to prayer for support, the importance of not giving up when life becomes difficult, etc.

Thank you for being a blessing to me and everyone who has been around you. You will always live on in my heart, memory, and life. You are precious to me and I love you.

Psalm 23: "The Lord is my shepherd, I shall not be in want. He makes me lie down in green pastures, he leads me beside quiet waters, he restores my soul. He guides me in paths of righteousness for his name's sake. Even though I walk through the valley of the shadow of death, I will fear no evil, for you are with me; your rod and your staff, they comfort me. You prepare a table before me in the presence of my enemies. You anoint my head with oil; my cup overflows. Surely goodness and love will follow me all the days of my life, and I will dwell in the house of the Lord forever."

Revelation 7:9–17: "After this I looked and there before me was a great multitude that no one could count, from every nation, tribe, people and language, standing before the throne and in front of the Lamb. They were wearing white robes and were holding palm branches in their hands. And they cried out in a loud voice: 'Salvation belongs to our God, who sits on the throne, and to the Lamb.' All the angels were standing around the throne and around the elders and the four living creatures. They fell down on their faces before the throne and worshiped God, saying: 'Amen! Praise and glory and wisdom and thanks and honor and power and strength be to our God for ever and ever. Amen!' Then one of the elders asked me, 'These in white robes—who are they, and where did they come from?' I answered, 'Sir, you know.' And he said, 'These are they who have come out of the great tribulation; they have washed their robes and made them white in the blood of the Lamb. Therefore, they are before the throne of God and serve him day and night in his temple; and he who sits on the throne will spread his tent over them. Never again will they hunger; never again will they thirst. The sun will not beat upon them, nor any scorching heat. For the Lamb at the center of the throne will be their shepherd; he will lead them to springs of living water. And God will wipe away every tear from their eyes.' "

John 14:1–6: "[Jesus states,] 'Do not let your hearts be troubled. Trust in God; trust also in me. In my Father's house are many rooms; if it were not so, I would have told you. I am going there to prepare a place for you. And if I go and prepare a place for you, I will come back and take you to be with me that you also may be where I am. You know the way to the place where I am going.' Thomas said to him, 'Lord, we don't know where you are going, so how can we know the way?' Jesus answered, 'I am the way and the truth and the life.' "

Pray *prior* to death. (Pray this or your own prayer.): In these last moments of my loved one's life, O God, I thank you for having given _____ to me as one of the dearest and most important persons in my life. She (He) has been a blessing and inspiration. As she (he) surrenders her (his) last breaths to you, comfort her (him) with your love and peace. We let her (him) go, trusting in your mercy. Comfort us also as we let go of one another. We turn to you for true peace. In Jesus' name. Amen.

Pray *after* death. (Pray this or your own prayer.): O merciful God, I commend my _____ to your eternal keeping. Receive this person who is so dear to me into your glorious kingdom so that she (he) may rest in your love, peace, and joy forever. I love you and place my faith and trust in your goodness. Bestow now your compassion upon her (him), just as you share your tenderness with me during this sacred time. In Jesus' name I pray. Amen.

The Lord's Prayer: Our Father, who art in heaven, hallowed be thy name, thy kingdom come, thy will be done, on earth as it is in heaven. Give us this day our daily bread; and forgive us our trespasses, as we forgive those who trespass against us; and lead us not into temptation, but deliver us from evil. For thine is the kingdom, and the power, and the glory, forever and ever. Amen.

Blessing: And now may the Lord bless us and keep us. The Lord make his face shine upon us and be gracious to us. The Lord look upon us with favor and give us peace. In the name of the Father, and of the Son, and of the Holy Spirit. Amen.

After your loved one's spirit has departed this world, spend as much time as you like with his body. Do not allow anyone to rush you into calling the mortician. Spend time alone with him as the finality of his death becomes real for you. Turn off equipment in the room so that it is quieter. If your loved one dies in a nursing home or hospital, the staff may ask you to step out of the room momentarily so they can tend to your loved one. You may want to ask the medical staff questions about the last minutes of your loved one's life or about the cause of death. If other family members are present, all of you may benefit by telling stories about your loved one's life.

If your loved one died when you were out of the room or before you arrived, remember that no one dies alone. God is present.

Again, remain with your loved one who has died as long as you wish. Say your good-bye. Do not rush away—and later regret it. Feel free to touch your loved one after he has died—hold his hand, give him a kiss, rub his forehead, and/or give him a final hug.

If your loved one died in an institution, follow the lead of the professional staff regarding procedures at the time of death. If you have not already given the staff the name of your loved one's preferred funeral home, you will be asked for this information. Tell the staff not to call the funeral home until you are almost ready to leave. Do not allow the staff to hurry you. This is your last sacred moment with your loved one.

After your loved one's death, an institutional representative may ask you to sign papers. Make sure you know what you are signing.

Hospital staff may request that you sign a permission form to perform an autopsy or to harvest organs for donation. Know your loved one's wishes. Refer to his health care directive. Do not allow the medical staff to force you to donate organs or to allow an autopsy if it was against your loved one's wishes. If you would like an autopsy to answer specific personal questions, keep in mind that you can restrict the autopsy to certain areas or organs of the body. If you do not restrict the autopsy, a full body autopsy will be done. Always inquire whether you will be charged a fee for the autopsy.

Also in a hospital or care facility, you will be given your loved one's personal belongings and asked to sign a form indicating that you received them. Only sign the form if you are certain that you have received all the items. A hospital should have a list of the items your loved one brought. Pay special attention to jewelry, money, hearing aids, eyeglasses, a personal Bible, and other cherished keepsakes.

A nursing home will give you a timeline by which you are required to remove your loved one's personal possessions, including furniture brought from home. When you leave the nursing home after the death, take home as many valuables as possible so that they are not misplaced or stolen before you return.

When you have said your final good-bye to your loved one, give the staff permission to call the mortician. You may want to remain until the mortician arrives so that you can schedule an appointment for the next day, ask initial questions, or again say good-bye to your loved one. Questions for the funeral director can be asked, of course, over the telephone if you prefer to leave before the mortician arrives.

WORKING WITH THE MORTICIAN AND PASTOR

Prior to making arrangements for a funeral or memorial service, locate a copy of your loved one's Preplanning Your Funeral or Memorial Service Form (appendix B) and other important papers that you might need. Hopefully, you know exactly where to find them. If not, look for them in your loved one's Bible, files, desk, attaché case, refrigerator, or any other places where she normally placed important documents. Also look in her bank safe-deposit box.

If your loved one's pastor was not present at the time of death, telephone to inform her or him of the death. Inquire about the pastor's and church's availability for the funeral or memorial service. Make an appointment to meet with the pastor.

During your visit with the pastor, inquire about the order and content of the funeral service. Take an active part in planning the service, using your loved one's Preplanning Your Funeral or Memorial Service Form. Remember that the service does not have to be totally sad. It can be a time to celebrate God's gift of eternal life, your loved one's life, and your loved one's spiritual legacy, as well as a time to acknowledge your grief and need for God's ongoing comfort and strength.

Tell the pastor about your loved one and how important she was to you. The better the pastor knows your loved one (and you), the more meaningful the funeral service will be. During the service, you or other persons who were close to your loved one may want to say a few words, read a poem, read Scripture, or provide special music. If you decide to speak during the service, write down what you want to say and ask someone to be your backup in case it becomes too emotionally difficult to follow through. The pastor may be willing to do so.

When visiting the funeral home, remember that the mortician works for you—not the other way around. Your loved one's preferences (and yours) take precedence. Bring your loved one's Preplanning Your Funeral or Memorial Service Form as well as the Care Recipient's Information Form (appendices A and B), which include her Social Security number, record of military service, and the name of a charitable organization or cause to which people can send contributions. It is acceptable to designate memorial gifts for funeral expenses. You can bring your loved one's burial clothes to the mortuary during your initial visit or at another time.

A word of caution: Do not allow someone from the mortuary to pressure you into buying the most expensive casket in the showroom. Before you go into the showroom (unless you have previously made your selection), look at the price list of caskets and vaults so that you have control over which ones to allow the mortician to show you. The casket is usually the most expensive item for a funeral. The funeral home is required to allow you to use a casket you may have purchased elsewhere. If you prefer cremation, the funeral home cannot require you to purchase a casket.

Prior to making decisions about professional services available through the mortician, also request to see a price list that includes outside persons and organizations that you will need to pay, such as the cemetery association, florists, newspapers for death and funeral notices, musicians, clergy, and caterers. Rely upon the mortician for assistance in obtaining these services as well as obtaining death certificates, audio- or videotaping the funeral/memorial service, and contacting insurance companies and the military regarding financial assistance.

In addition to scheduling the actual service, options are available for visitation at the funeral home. You can schedule private individual time with your loved one's body, private family time with your loved one, and public time when others come to say good-bye to your loved one and express their condolences to you. A private or public prayer service led by the pastor can be scheduled for the evening prior to the funeral service if the pastor is available. Although visitation times at the funeral home involve additional fees, they are an important part of your grief process because these times help you to emotionally accept the fact of your loved one's death, to spiritually prepare for the funeral or memorial service, to share your grief feelings with others who knew your loved one, and to receive support and comfort from people who care about you.

GOD'S PEACE IS WITH YOU

Caregivers, don't lose heart. Jesus promised eternal life to all who trust in him. Eternal life through Jesus Christ is the goal we look forward to in the future as well as the meaning that brings all of life together at the end. Thank God for blessing you with the guidance, strength, and ability to fulfill your spiritual calling to love and honor your care recipient while she was on earth and as she transcended into eternity. Well done, good and faithful servant. Be at peace. And remember, God continues to be with you.

SCRIPTURE

"After the Sabbath, at dawn on the first day of the week, Mary Magdalene and the other Mary went to look at the tomb. There was a violent earthquake,

for an angel of the Lord came down from heaven and, going to the tomb, rolled back the stone and sat on it. His appearance was like lightning, and his clothes were white as snow. The guards were so afraid of him that they shook and became like dead men. The angel said to the women, 'Do not be afraid, for I know that you are looking for Jesus, who was crucified. He is not here; he has risen, just as he said. Come and see the place where he lay. Then go quickly and tell his disciples: "He has risen from the dead and is going ahead of you into Galilee. There you will see him." Now I have told you.' So the women hurried away from the tomb, afraid yet filled with joy, and ran to tell his disciples. Suddenly Jesus met them. 'Greetings,' he said. They came to him, clasped his feet and worshiped him. Then Jesus said to them, 'Do not be afraid. Go and tell my brothers to go to Galilee; there they will see me' " (Matthew 28:1–10).

"We know that the one who raised the Lord Jesus from the dead will also raise us with Jesus" (2 Corinthians 4:14).

PRAYERS

Caregiver's Prayer Prior to Loved One's Death

O God, my loved one is nearing the time of death. Help me to speak tender, assuring words of love to her (him), as well as to perform comfort cares that help her (him) to rest well. Grant the health care workers the ability and desire to keep my loved one comfortable and free of pain. Help me to give my loved one permission to let go of life on earth. I thank you for having given her (him) to me as one of the dearest and most important persons in my life. She (he) has been a blessing and inspiration. I thank you that your resurrection promise has the last word in our lives. I commend my loved one to you now. I also ask you to comfort and strengthen me during this sacred time. In Jesus' name. Amen.

Caregiver's Prayer After Death

O God, I need you. Now that my loved one and I have gone through the caregiving journey and the sacred moment of death, I am filled with feelings of deep grief and loss. I can only get through my emptiness with you at my side, comforting me, strengthening me, and filling me with your peace. Don't let me lose heart. Sustain me with your divine compassion and love. I need you. Amen.

Chapter Thirteen
Comfort and Support in Your Bereavement

Your life is different now. Your care recipient has died. You cared for him well. You have no doubt invested enormous time, energy, and personal sacrifice into loving and honoring him. Now you are without your loved one and you feel alone. Your life is different. This is what is meant by bereavement.

Many books have been written about bereavement. This chapter does not attempt to replicate them. Instead, this chapter briefly describes normal feelings of bereavement for caregivers, makes suggestions for how to go on with life after your loved one's death, and uplifts you spiritually as you do so. Because visiting your loved one's final resting place (cemetery, mausoleum, etc.) is important for your grief process, this chapter also includes a "Visiting the Final Resting Place Service" that you can use when you return to the place of interment.

FEELINGS OF THE BEREAVED PERSON

Although each bereaved person grieves in a different way, the following feelings are normal; therefore, be assured there is nothing wrong with you if you experience some of them.

Gratitude. You are grateful that God blessed you with a close relationship with your loved one—and that you were able to be an attentive and devoted caregiver when your loved one developed limitations in life. You also are grateful that God's promise of eternal life comforts you and fills you with hope as you continue your journey on earth.

Fear. Now that your loved one has died, you fear that you will never get over your grief: never stop crying, never get on with your life with renewed purpose and meaning, never survive without your loved one, and never again have a person in your life who will love you as unconditionally, comfort you as genuinely, and advise you as wisely as she did. You also fear that one day you will develop the same physical limitations and medical conditions that led to her eventual death.

Depression and loneliness. You feel sad, abandoned, orphaned, and alone. Your future feels hopeless and empty without your loved one who has died. You sit and stare, eat improperly (if at all), and choose not to exercise. Your depressed feelings ruminate in your mind and heart—they never seem to stop. You see no light at the end of the tunnel. You do not think the sun will ever shine again in your life.

Guilt. While you, of course, obtained competent medical care for your loved one, you feel guilty that you did not obtain the world's best medical care, even though that would have involved extensive travel and expense that neither your loved one nor you could afford. You also feel guilty that sometimes you became out-of-sorts with your loved one, wished your caregiving experience was over (because it took a tremendous emotional and physical toll on you), longed for fun and recreation (because you missed having your own life), and possibly prayed for your loved one to die—due to her low-quality life and suffering.

Relief. You feel relieved now that you can rest from the enormous stress of caregiving, that you are no longer (hopefully) being criticized by an ungrateful family member or even your care recipient, that your loved one's suffering is over, and that you can reclaim your life. A weight is lifted off your shoulders.

Anger. You may feel angry at your loved one for dying and leaving you, at the doctors and medical staff for not doing more to cure her or better care for her, at relatives who did not help or support you with the caregiving tasks, and at the overall situation that caused you to lose work time, financial savings, and personal time.

Preoccupation with memories of your loved one. Because you deeply miss your loved one, you long to see and talk with her again. Your preoccupation leads you to think you see or hear her during the daytime, and you dream about her at night. You refuse to allow yourself to let go of your thoughts about her because you worry that if you do, you will no longer remember everything about her.

Idealization. Now that your loved one has died, you idealize her personality and life, as well as focus exclusively upon her positive traits, values, and legacy. Keep in mind that no one is perfect. Everyone has shortcomings—and that includes your loved one, just as it includes you.

Helplessness and confusion. You feel at loose ends. You are confused about how to return to loving and caring for yourself. Give yourself permission to prepare your favorite entrees (rather than those that were required for your loved one's diet), to appreciate uninterrupted meals, to eat in your favorite restaurant, to sleep whenever you are tired, to take your time with paper work (because you no longer have a multitude of caregiving tasks to do), to engage in pleasurable forms of recreation, and to become accustomed to silence without wondering when the next crisis will occur.

Inability to concentrate. At times you are temporarily absent-minded and other times (both at home and at work) you engage in circular thinking. Your thoughts are like a boomerang—they always return to your loved one and your caregiving experience. You struggle to concentrate on anything else. Yes, this is normal. Give yourself time to heal.

Tears. Tears sneak up on you when you least expect them, such as when you hear your loved one's favorite song on the car radio, see her favorite food items when you shop for groceries, see her favorite flowers, channel-surf and come to her favorite television program, catch yourself saying something that she would have said, shop in a department store and see something on display that she would have liked, get in your car and absentmindedly drive to the pharmacy for her medications, or pick up the telephone to call her. Well-known author Washington Irving very eloquently described the relationship between tears and grief in these words: "There is a sacredness in tears. They are not the mark of weakness, but of power. They speak more eloquently than ten thousand tongues. They are messengers of overwhelming grief . . . and unspeakable love."[1]

Physical symptoms frequently accompany grief feelings. Some common symptoms include loss of energy, restlessness, gastrointestinal problems, shortness of breath, sighing, sleep problems, pacing, staring, weakness, tearfulness, and numbness. A visit to your physician will put your mind at ease so that your imagination does not cause you to believe you have developed a serious medical condition.

TAKE TIME TO GRIEVE AND HEAL

Remember that the third part of your threefold spiritual calling is to love yourself. As you grieve, treat yourself as kindly as you would treat your best friend in a similar situation. Love yourself by giving yourself permission and time to grieve. Refer to chapters 3 and 4 for spiritual and psychological nurturing tips. Join a grief support group where you can talk about how you feel and hear from others how they feel and cope with similar experiences. Find or make a place of refuge where you can remember your loved one, grieve his passing, and heal. Such healing can take place as you sit in your prayer corner or in your loved one's favorite room or chair, ride your bicycle, walk through a beautiful park, view paintings in your favorite art gallery, attend concerts, or visit your loved one's final resting place.

As you take time to grieve, some of the following things may help you to heal:[2]

- Look at a photo album and remember positive experiences you had with your loved one. View family videotapes.

- Display cherished gifts from your loved one.

- Play music that reminds you of him.

- Write down your feelings.

- Say your loved one's name out loud a number of times.

- Place flowers at his final resting place.

- Cook your loved one's favorite food as a way of cherishing his memory and use a special bowl or piece of silverware from your loved one for your meal.

- Accept invitations and tasks only as you have the energy to do so. Listen to your heart. You will not always feel the way you do now, so do not force yourself to do something you do not want to do.

- Give yourself permission to enjoy activities and companionship, if you so desire. Your loved one would want you to have a fulfilling and blessed life.

- Recognize how far you have come. Give thanks for the special strength you have found within yourself. Congratulate yourself for getting out of bed on the days when doing so seemed impossible. Give yourself credit for learning to manage the everyday stuff of life without your loved one.

- Lower your expectations of yourself and be flexible.

Wave after wave of finality may come upon you at different times and in different places. Just as God was with you when you took care of your loved one, God continues to be with you as you take time to grieve and heal.

GETTING ON WITH YOUR LIFE

Only you will know when it is time to get on with your life. Remember that your loved one's death is not the end of your life. You have a life ahead of you. As you begin to move forward, ask God to guide you. Consider the following suggestions as you regroup. Work on one suggestion at a time or on all of them together.

Reorder your daily routine and goals. During your caregiving experience, you balanced caregiving, personal family responsibilities (in some cases), and perhaps employment. Whether you were an in-home caregiver, nearby caregiver, or long-distance caregiver, you became an expert in daily time management. Your reason to get up in the morning was to care for your loved one. Now you need to establish a new reason for getting up in the morning. Your initial reason to get up might be just to make it through the new day. Make a list of things you need and want to do each day. Begin with small goals and gradually increase them as you are ready and able. Prioritize the goals on your list and check them off when they are completed.

Continue to live out your spiritual calling. God continues to give you a threefold spiritual calling in life: to love God, neighbor, and self. Pray about how God wants you to live out your threefold spiritual calling now. Write down the insights God gives you as well as the philosophies by which you lived prior to caregiving. Ask yourself what kind of person God wants you to be and what kind of person you want to be as you continue to follow your spiritual calling. Take heart and remember: You are important to God.

Adopt parts of your loved one's spiritual legacy. As you get on with your life, adopt parts of your loved one's spiritual legacy to your life. Review her spiritual legacy as she articulated it to you when you used conversation topics from the Spiritual Journey Exercise for Individuals found in appendix D. Also review the letter of gratitude you wrote and shared with her before she died. Reflect upon positive attributes you want to remember about your loved one, such as her special virtues, values, philosophy of life, spiritual beliefs, and how she shared love and affection with you and other people. As you incorporate her special attributes into your life, your loved one's life becomes a living memorial through which you keep alive the essence of her being.

WHEN SOMEONE ASKS, "WHAT CAN I DO?"

Be honest with people who want to help you. You need help in getting through your bereavement. When they ask how they can help you, tell them what you need. They will be grateful for your suggestions. When they ask, you may want to respond in some of the following ways:

- Realize that the death of my loved one is very difficult, even though I anticipated his death for quite some time and he was advanced in years. I miss him in every aspect of life, and my life is very different now. It would help a lot if you would just invite me to talk about him and about how I miss him.

- Will you give me a hug? I need to know someone is here for me because I feel so alone. I'll be getting better, but for now I need support.

- Remember me on the anniversary date of my loved one's death and on holidays. Telephone me and see how I am doing.

- Pray for me—and if you say you will pray for me, please do so. Your prayers will give me strength, guidance, and hope.

- Please go with me to the cemetery and join me as I use the "Visiting the Final Resting Place Service." (The service is found later in this chapter.)

- Remind me to prepare meals and eat; and, when you have time, perhaps we could go out to eat or go out for coffee. Occasionally invite me to go with you for a walk or a bike ride.

- Encourage me to smile and laugh again.

SPIRITUAL NURTURE

God's love through Jesus Christ will sustain you in your time of bereavement. This is not a platitude—this is a fact. Believe it!

God understands your emotional pain better than anyone else can—and gives you strength to get through your grief. He says to you: "Fear not. . . . When you pass through the waters, I will be with you; and when you pass through the rivers, they will not sweep over you. . . . I am the Lord, your God. . . . You are precious . . . I love you. . . . I am with you" (Isaiah 43:1–5).

God's Son, Jesus, who himself greatly suffered on earth, says: "Come to me, all you who are weary and burdened, and I will give you rest. . . . I am gentle and humble in heart, and you will find rest for your souls" (Matthew 11:28–29). Yes, God walks with you in your bereavement—and comforts and strengthens you so that you can survive it.

Make yourself available to receive God's comfort and strength by regularly praying, reading the Bible, and attending worship services. During prayer time at home, include quiet time to be with God and to listen to God. As you read Scripture, focus upon passages of love, strength, guidance, comfort, and peace (many of which are found at the end of each chapter and in appendix E). When you worship with your favorite congregation, allow the love of God in his holy sanctuary to touch your heart and soul.

If necessary, write "prayer time," "Bible reading time," and "worship time" in your appointment book or on your wall calendar. God, of course, comforts you twenty-four hours each day, but as you make specific time for God, the Holy Spirit draws you even closer to him. Review chapter 3 for helpful ways to nurture your relationship with God.

Grieve as a person of hope. Do not wonder if God will do something to help you, because God has already done something very powerful to help you. He gave his only Son, Jesus, who suffered and died for you—and overcame the power of death for you. Just as God rolled away the stone from the tomb on Jesus' resurrection day, thereby promising new life to the world, God rolls the stone away from the hole of your grief and gives you a future filled with renewed life.

God's intention is for you to make it through your grief experience. Just as there is no end to God's power to help you heal, there is no end to your privilege to draw upon his love. The apostle Paul wrote, "Thanks be to God, who gives us the victory [over death] through our Lord Jesus Christ" (1 Corinthians 15:57 NRSV). The wonderful thing about God's victory over death is not how well you hang on to God, but how powerfully God hangs on to you. God will not allow you to lose heart!

VISITING THE FINAL RESTING PLACE

Use this service as often as you wish. You may find the "Visiting the Final Resting Place Service" especially helpful one week after your loved one's death, one month after the death, on the anniversary of your loved one's birthday, on Memorial Day, for the one-year anniversary of the death, and at other significant times.

As you engage in this service, you may want to bring flowers, a candle and matches, a CD player and music, and a folding chair. At times you may prefer to go through this service by yourself, while other times you may want to invite another family member or a friend to join you. As you go through this service, feel free to modify, paraphrase, and adapt it to your personal situation.

Visiting the Final Resting Place Service

Invocation:

I begin in the name of the Father, and of the Son, and of the Holy Spirit.

Opening Prayer:

O God of the living, whose own Son, Jesus, died and rose again, hear my prayer this day as I come to my loved one's holy resting place, giving thanks for _____ and for the many ways she (he) touched my life. I also thank you for the promise of eternal life for all who believe in Jesus Christ, in whose name I pray. Amen.

Lighting of Candle:

As I light this candle in my loved one's memory, I give thanks that she (he) helped light my way on earth. Now I ask you to continue to light my way, guide my life, and fill me with your peace.

Listen to a piece of music that your loved one enjoyed.

Selected Bible Readings:

The Twenty-third Psalm:

"The Lord is my shepherd, I shall not be in want. He makes me lie down in green pastures, he leads me beside quiet waters, he restores my soul. He guides me in paths of righteousness for his name's sake. Even though I walk through the valley of the shadow of death, I will fear no evil, for you are with me; your rod and your staff, they comfort me. You prepare a table before me in the presence of my enemies. You anoint my head with oil; my cup overflows. Surely goodness and love will follow me all the days of my life, and I will dwell in the house of the Lord forever."

Matthew 5:4:

"Blessed are those who mourn, for they will be comforted."

1 Thessalonians 4:13–14:

"We do not want you to be ignorant about those who fall asleep, or to grieve like the rest . . . who have no hope. We believe that Jesus died and rose again and so we believe that God will bring with Jesus those who have fallen asleep in him."

John 3:16:
"For God so loved the world that he gave his one and only Son, that whoever believes in him shall not perish but have eternal life."

Romans 8:38–39:
"For I am convinced that neither death nor life, neither angels nor demons, neither the present nor the future, nor any powers, neither height nor depth, nor anything else in all creation, will be able to separate us from the love of God that is in Christ Jesus our Lord."

Matthew 11:28–29:
"Come to me, all you who are weary and burdened, and I will give you rest. Take my yoke upon you and learn from me, for I am gentle and humble in heart, and you will find rest for your souls."

Listen to a piece of music that you enjoy.

Sharing of Memories and Feelings:
As I pause and meditate, I recall the memories and feelings I have about my loved one's death. [Time for reflection—and conversation (if others also take part in the service).]

Prayer (or one of your own):
As I grieve, O God, help me to express all my feelings. Sometimes I misinterpret my feelings of grief. Although I know that they are normal, sometimes in my confusion I forget and think that they are abnormal, especially when they are accompanied by physical symptoms. Grief is not easy. Help me to take positive steps to love and care for myself, such as resting, eating nutritiously, exercising, listening to favorite music, being with supportive people whom I enjoy, visiting with my pastor (if you have one), talking with a therapist, participating in a support group, reading my Bible, attending worship services, and doing other things that will get me through this difficult time. Most

of all, help me to make time for you and sit quietly in your presence. Comfort me with your love and fill me with your heavenly peace. In Jesus' name I pray. Amen.

Time for Quiet Reflection

Closing Prayer (or one of your own):
O God, today is a day of memories. My loved one's death was a day of deep sorrow. I feel a profound sense of loss. I am grateful to you for having given me such a good and loving _____. I take delight in my memories of the good and meaningful times that we experienced together. May this time of prayerful remembrance at her (his) final resting place help me to remember that my ultimate comfort and strength come from your promise of eternal life. As I continue to grieve, comfort me with your divine peace. I pray through Jesus Christ our Lord. Amen.

Benediction:
The Lord bless me and keep me. The Lord make his face shine upon me and be gracious to me. The Lord look upon me with favor and give me peace. In the name of the Father, and of the Son, and of the Holy Spirit. Amen.

Close by listening to a favorite piece of music.

One-Year Anniversary of Death

Mark the one-year anniversary of your loved one's death in a special way. Decide whether you want to spend the day alone, with friends, or with family members. At mealtime, prepare your loved one's favorite entree and use a piece of her china or silverware. Again (if possible) visit your loved one's resting place and engage in the "Visiting the Final Resting Place Service." Substitute the following petition for the Closing Prayer:

Dear God, today is a day of memories for me. One year ago my loved one died. Her (his) passing was a time of both sorrow and hope. My heart still cries tears of loss. I tried diligently to be a devoted, loving, and competent caregiver. Thank you for always guiding me on my caregiving journey. I continue to thank you for the gifts you gave to us, especially the gift of each other. We learned from each other and faced life together. I treasure our time together. The memories I have will be with me forever because my loved one's life made my existence richer and more fulfilling. Help me always to incorporate the most positive and meaningful parts of her (his) spiritual legacy into my spiritual calling.

On this anniversary of her (his) death, I am mindful that as I cared for my loved one at the end of her (his) life, I also was learning how to approach my own death. I pray that I will approach the end of my life graciously, through my trust in your compassionate love. Fill me with your divine peace, today and every day. Thank you. Amen.

SCRIPTURE

"When Jesus saw the crowds, he went up the mountain; and after he sat down, his disciples came to him. Then he began to speak, and taught them, saying: 'Blessed are the poor in spirit, for theirs is the kingdom of heaven. Blessed are those who mourn, for they will be comforted. Blessed are the meek, for they will inherit the earth. Blessed are those who hunger and thirst for righteousness, for they will be filled. Blessed are the merciful, for they will receive mercy. Blessed are the pure in heart, for they will see God. Blessed are the peacemakers, for they will be called children of God' " (Matthew 5:1–9 NRSV).

PRAYER

God, you have called your servants to ventures of which we cannot see the ending, by paths as yet untrodden, through perils unknown. Give us faith to go out with good courage, not knowing where we go, but only that your hand is leading us and your love supporting us; through Jesus Christ our Lord. Amen.[3]

Appendix A: Care Recipient Information Form

This form should be completed before your care recipient experiences serious medical problems. Upon completion, place one copy in your home, one copy in your loved one's home, and one copy in the glove compartment of each motor vehicle so that it can be easily accessed in an emergency. Continually update the information and date each new entry.

Date _____

Name of Person(s) Who Completed This Form _____

Name of Care Recipient _____

Address _____

Home Telephone Number _____

E-mail Address _____

LOCATION OF IMPORTANT PAPERS

Birth certificate _____

Marriage certificate _____

Divorce papers _____

Social Security card (and number) _____

Passport _____

Driver's license (and number) _____

Citizenship papers _____

Adoption papers _____

Military record _____

Will and trusts _____

Health Care Directive (Living Will) _____

Safe-deposit box _____

Post office box _____

Preplanning Your Funeral or Memorial Service Form _____

Power of Attorney Form _____

MEDICAL INFORMATION

Medicare or Medicaid Number _____

Medicare Supplement Insurance Company, Policy Number, and How
to Contact _____

_____

Long-Term Care Insurance Company, Policy Number, and How to
Contact _____

_____

Private Health Insurance Company, Policy Number, and How to
Contact _____

_____

Dental Insurance Company, Policy Number, and How to Contact

_____

_____

Disability Insurance Company, Policy Number, and How to Contact

_____

Name of Preferred Hospital, Address, and Telephone Number

_____

_____

Name of Preferred Nursing Home, Address, and Telephone Number

_____

_____

Name of Preferred Hospice Organization, Address, and Telephone
Number _____

_____

Name of Physicians, Addresses, and Telephone Numbers

1. _____

_____

2. _____

_____

3. _____

_____

Name of Dentist, Address, and Telephone Number

_____

_____

Names of Pharmacies, Addresses, and Telephone Numbers

1. _____

_____

2. _____

_____

3. Mail Order Pharmacy _____

_____

Name of Physical Therapist, Address, and Telephone Number

_____

_____

Name of Home Health Care Agency, Address, and Telephone Number

_____

_____

Name of Hairstylist, Address, and Telephone Number

_____

_____

Name, Address, and Telephone Number of Health Care Agent

_____

_____

Prescribed Medications, Including Dosage, Where Purchased, and Schedule

1. _____
2. _____
3. _____
4. _____
5. _____
6. _____
7. _____
8. _____

Over-the-Counter Medications (including vitamins), Dosage, and Schedule

1. _____

2. _____

3. _____

4. _____

5. _____

6. _____

7. _____

8. _____

Dates of Immunizations

1. Flu Shot _____

2. Pneumonia Shot _____

3. Tetanus Shot _____

4. _____

5. _____

Dates of Health Screenings

1. Diabetes _____

2. Cholesterol _____

3. _____

4. _____

5. _____

Dates, Types, and Locations of Surgeries

1. _____

2. _____

3. _____

4. _____

5. _____

Other Hospitalizations, Dates, and Locations

1. _____

2. _____

3. _____

4. _____

5. _____

Medical Challenges

1. _____   6. _____

2. _____   7. _____

3. _____   8. _____

4. _____   9. _____

5. _____   10. _____

Blood Type _____

Psychological Challenges (e.g., claustrophobia—needs the door open; panic attacks—needs metered counting; anxiety—needs slowness and calmness)

1. _____

2. _____

3. _____

4. _____

5. _____

Communication Challenges (e.g., impaired speech, cognitive challenges, vision or hearing deficiency)

1. _____

2. _____

3. _____

4. _____

5. _____

Favorite Foods (breakfast, lunch, dinner, snacks)

1. _____   6. _____

2. _____   7. _____

3. _____   8. _____

4. _____   9. _____

5. _____   10. _____

Food Allergies

1. _____   3. _____

2. _____   4. _____

Food Dislikes

1. _____   3. _____

2. _____   4. _____

HOUSEHOLD

Location of House Keys _____

Location of Car Keys _____

Location of Safe-Deposit Box Key _____

Location of Utility Bills and Related Paper Work _____

Location of House Deed and Abstract _____

Name of Plumber and Telephone Number _____

Name of Gardener and Telephone Number _____

Name of Electrician and Telephone Number _____

Name of Cleaning Person _____

Name of Homeowner's Insurance Company, Address, Telephone Number, and Policy Number _____

FINANCIAL

Names of Banks, Addresses, Telephone Numbers, and Account Numbers

1. _____

_____

2. _____

_____

3. _____

_____

Name of Mortgage Company, Address, Telephone Number, and Account Number

_____

_____

Name of Credit Card Companies, Addresses, Telephone Numbers, and Account Numbers

1. _____

_____

2. _____

_____

3. _____

_____

4. _____

_____

5. _____

_____

Name of Stock Brokers and Financial Advisors, Addresses, Telephone Numbers, and Account Numbers

1. _____

_____

2. _____

_____

3. _____

_____

4. _____

_____

5. _____

_____

Name of Pension Companies, Addresses, Telephone Numbers, and Account Numbers

1. _____

_____

2. _____

3. _____

_____

Name of Automobile Insurance Company, Address, Telephone Number, and Policy Number _____

_____

Location of Automobile Title and Other Title Cards _____

_____

Name of Life Insurance Company, Address, Telephone Number, and Policy Number

_____

_____

Name of Tax Preparer, Address, and Telephone Number _____

_____

Location of Precious Jewelry, Coins, Stamps, etc. _____

_____

OTHER

Name of Clergyperson and Congregation, Address, and Telephone Number _____

_____

Name of Attorney, Address, and Telephone Number _____

_____

Names of Family Caregivers, Addresses, and Telephone Numbers

1. _____

_____

2. _____

_____

3. _____

_____

4. _____

_____

Names of Close Friends, Addresses, and Telephone Numbers

1. _____

_____

2. _____

_____

3. _____

_____

Names of Helpful Neighbors, Addresses, and Telephone Numbers

1. _____

_____

2. _____

_____

3. _____

_____

Appendix B: Preplanning Your Funeral or Memorial Service Form

Encourage your care recipient to use this form to plan her (his) funeral or memorial service. Have your loved one sign and date this form. Your loved one may change anything on the form at any time. When she (he) does, notify each person and organization that has a copy of your original form. Also date the changes. Your loved one's signature indicates her (his) hope that the preferences will be fulfilled as closely as possible. Spouses should each fill out a separate form.

Name (printed) _____

Address _____

Telephone Number _____

Signature _____

Date _____

Contact Person _____

Telephone Number _____

Contact's Address _____

E-mail Address _____

Distribute copies of this form:

- Keep one copy for yourself.
- Give one copy to each of your children, if you have children.
- Give one copy to your church office, where it will be placed in a confidential file and will be immediately available when needed.
- Give one copy to your preferred funeral home.
- Give one copy to the person who holds power of attorney.

PERSONAL INFORMATION

Date and Place of Birth _____

Names of Parents _____

Name (Maiden) of Spouse _____

Date and Place of Marriage _____

Names of Previous Spouses _____

Names of Children, Including Addresses and Telephone Numbers

1. _____

_____

2. _____

_____

3. _____

_____

4. _____

_____

5. _____

_____

Names of Siblings, Including Addresses and Telephone Numbers

1. _____

   _____

2. _____

   _____

3. _____

   _____

4. _____

   _____

5. _____

   _____

Number of Grandchildren: _____

Number of Great-grandchildren: _____

Names of Other Significant Relatives, Including Addresses and Telephone Numbers

1. _____

   _____

2. _____

   _____

Names of Close Friends to Contact, Including Addresses and Telephone Numbers

1. _____

   _____

2. _____

   _____

3. _____

_____

Mother's Full Name (Maiden) and Birthplace _____

_____

Father's Full Name and Birthplace _____

Occupations/Types of Business/Employers, Including Dates

1. _____

2. _____

3. _____

4. _____

5. _____

Military Service, Including Branch and Dates _____

_____

Education (Institutions Attended and Degrees Received)

1. _____

2. _____

3. _____

4. _____

Professional, Fraternal, and Community Organization Memberships

_____

_____

_____

Hobbies and Interests _____

_____

Organ Donation? Yes _____   No _____

If yes, the following organs or tissues only _____

_____

RELIGIOUS INFORMATION

Date and Place of Baptism _____

Date and Place of Confirmation _____

Congregations (and locations) in which you have been a member

1. _____

   _____

2. _____

   _____

3. _____

   _____

Areas of Church Involvement

_____

_____

_____

_____

Preferred Hymns/Songs

Processional: _____

Recessional: _____

Other: _____

_____

_____

Possible Hymns:
"A Mighty Fortress"
"My Hope is Built on Nothing Less"
"O God, Our Help in Ages Past"
"Rock of Ages"
"Jesus, Still Lead On"
"Oh, Happy Day, When We Shall Stand"
"I Know That My Redeemer Lives"
"What a Friend We Have in Jesus"
"Amazing Grace"
"The King of Love My Shepherd Is"
"Beautiful Savior"
"How Great Thou Art"
"Now Thank We All Our God"
"This Is My Father's World"
"Blessed Assurance"
"Softly and Tenderly Jesus Is Calling"
"I Was There to Hear Your Borning Cry"
"You Who Dwell in the Shelter of the Lord" ("On Eagle's Wings")
"God Will Take Care of You"
"Precious Lord, Take My Hand"
"Be Still, My Soul"
"The Lord's My Shepherd"
"All the Way My Savior Leads Me"
"Christ Is Risen, Christ Is Living"
"The Old Rugged Cross"

Scripture Readings (Leave lines blank if you would like the pastor to select them.)

_____

_____

_____

These Scripture readings are meaningful to me because _____

_____

Names of Preferred Readers, Addresses, Telephone Numbers

_____

_____

_____

Special Music (Vocal or instrumental)

Name of Musician, Address, Telephone Number, and Type of Music _____

_____

_____

Title of Musical Selection(s)

1. _____

_____

2. _____

_____

3. _____

_____

This music is meaningful to me because _____

_____

_____

Names of Pallbearers

1. _____   4. _____

2. _____   5. _____

3. _____   6. _____

Is there anything you *do not* want regarding your funeral/memorial service? _____

_____

_____

FUNERAL HOME INFORMATION

Preferred Funeral Home, Address, and Telephone Number _____

_____

Burial or Cremation? Burial _____ Cremation _____

Name and Address of Cemetery or Place of Interment _____

_____

Type of Casket: Steel _____ Precious metal _____

 Wood (and type of wood) _____

Type of Burial Clothing and Its Location _____

Type of Flowers for the Service _____

Name of Charity, Church, or Cause (including funeral expenses) to which monetary gifts are designated _____

Type of Cemetery Marker _____

If cremation, preference for disposition of ashes

Earth burial _____ Mausoleum entombment _____

Scattering _____ Location: _____

Keep at home _____ Other: _____

Names of Newspapers (including address and fax number), where obituary is to be sent

1. _____

   _____

2. _____

   _____

3. _____

_____

Other Preferences _____

_____

_____

PERSONAL LEGACY

Christian Values and Beliefs _____

_____

What Pleases Me Most About My Life_____

_____

Accomplishments _____

_____

Words of Wisdom for Survivors _____

_____

Final Message to Family and Friends _____

_____

Other Final Thoughts _____

_____

_____

Write Your Own Obituary (if you would like to do so).

_____

_____

_____

_____

_____

_____

_____

_____

_____

_____

_____

_____

_____

_____

Appendix C: Blessing of the New Home Service

The purpose of the Blessing of the New Home Service is to help our loved ones who move into a new home (apartment, assisted-living facility, nursing home, or other care facility) to realize that neither God nor their family caregivers will abandon them. My hope is that everyone who participates in this service will feel more at peace and develop a greater acceptance of the need to relocate. When deciding to use this service, keep in mind that if your loved one is resistant to living in a care facility, it may be best to delay the service until a later time. And if your loved one is quite forgetful, she (he) may not remember at a later time that the service was held, but at the moment of going through the service it can be meaningful for her (him). The service may not be appropriate for loved ones with advanced dementia. The service may be more helpful when it is led by someone else (other than you, the caregiver) such as a pastor, a facility chaplain, or a significant friend. Feel free to make any adaptations to the service that you wish.

Service Leader:

We are here today to bless [name]'s new home at [name of facility]. This may be a time of mixed feelings for you and for [name of family caregiver]. You may feel discouraged about your changing health that made it necessary to leave your home. You may feel anxious about what life will be like here, as you meet the staff and other residents and adjust to a new schedule. On the other hand, it may be a relief for you that now you do not need to be concerned with housecleaning, grocery shopping, cooking, knowing when to take your medications, or even doing your laundry. You also may feel safer because someone is here with you twenty-four hours a day. Whether it's daytime or nighttime, there is always someone available to help you. God also is with you, as he has always been.

[*The service leader lights a candle.*]

As I light this candle, think about God's love. God has promised that he loves us and will be with us always. This means that God is with you in your new home.

Scripture: Isaiah 43:1–5 (paraphrased)

But now thus says the Lord who created you and formed you, Do not fear, for I have redeemed you. I have called you by name, [name of loved one and name of family caregiver]. You are mine. When you pass through the waters, I will be with you; and through the rivers, they shall not overwhelm you. For I am the Lord your God, your Savior. You are precious in my sight, and honored, and I love you. Do not fear, for I am with you.

Prayer (pray this prayer or your own prayer):

Our gracious God, we pray that you will bless [name of care recipient and name of family caregiver] and this new home with your divine presence. Help them to turn to you and to those around them in trust and hope. Give them strength to accept this change in their lives. Guide them to find meaning and goodness in life as they remember that you love them and that they belong to you; through Jesus Christ we pray. Amen.

Staff member (if available): (The staff member should feel free to improvise her own words)

My name is _____. I work as a _____. On behalf of the staff, I welcome you to our [name of facility] family. You are a unique creation of God, and you no doubt have special needs and wishes. We as a staff want you to know that we will care for you well. We invite all of you to let us know how you feel and what you need. We hope that the transition will be as easy as possible for each of you. God's blessing be with you in your new home here. [The staff person shakes hands with the resident.]

Tenant or resident of the facility (if available): (The words may be improvised)

My name is _____. On behalf of the tenants (residents) at [name of facility], I welcome you as a new friend, and look forward to having you join us for conversation, meals, and activities. May you be blessed through the friendships you make here and the new opportunities that you will enjoy here. [The resident shakes hands with the new resident.]

Family member(s):

I (We) know this is a difficult adjustment for you, [name]. It is also difficult for me (us). It is not easy. I (We) will continue to be here for you, just as I (we) was (were) with you in the past. I (We) love you. (Family members are encouraged to add words of their own. Family members give their loved one a hug or gentle squeeze of her hand.)

Facility chaplain (if available): (Words may be improvised)

On behalf of the community of faith at [name of facility], I welcome you. While you and the other residents continue your church membership in your home congregations, I invite you also to worship here with us and attend our Bible studies. May you be blessed and continue to grow in faith here in our home. [The chaplain shakes hands with the new resident.]

Pastor, lay caregiver, or member of the care recipient's congregation: (Words may be improvised)

You are an important and valued member of our congregation. We look forward to visiting you here in your new home. Because we know it is difficult for you to attend worship in our congregation, we hope you will feel free to worship here. While you worship here, you will continue to be a member of our congregation. We will continue to visit you, share Communion with you, and support you in your faith. May you be blessed as you grow spiritually in your new home. [The pastor or lay caregiver shakes hands with the member.]

Recorded Hymn: "O God, Our Help in Ages Past"

Service Leader:

Just as was true of your previous home, [name], here at [name of facility] many areas of your new home are significant.

[*The service leader walks to the door.*]

At this door to your room we read from Psalm 121:8, "The Lord will keep your going out and your coming in from this time on and forevermore" (NRSV). Let us pray. O God, protect and guide [name] as she (he) enters and leaves her (his) room. Make all her (his) comings and goings pleasant experiences. Through Jesus Christ our Lord we pray. Amen.

[*The service leader walks to the sitting area.*]

In this sitting area of your room we read from John 13:34, "I give you a new commandment, that you love one another. Just as I have loved you, you also should love one another" (NRSV). Let us pray. O God, bless all visits that [name] has with loved ones in her (his) room and over the telephone. May the visits be uplifting and encouraging, through Jesus Christ our Lord. Amen.

[*The service leader walks to the window.*]

In this area of light at the window of this room we read from John 8:12, "Jesus spoke to them, saying, 'I am the light of the world. Whoever follows me will never walk in darkness but will have the light of life' " (NRSV). Let us pray. O God, we give thanks for the light that comes into [name]'s home through this window. May this light remind her (him) of the hope and peace that you give her (him) each day, through Jesus Christ our Lord. Amen.

[*The service leader walks to the sleep area.*]

In this sleep area of your home we read from Psalm 4:8, "I will both lie down and sleep in peace; for you alone, O Lord, make me lie down in safety" (NRSV). Let us pray. O God, bless this sleep area so that it may be for [name] a place to fall asleep easily in your tender love and care, a place to sleep all through the night, and a place to arise rested and renewed for a new day with you; through Jesus Christ our Lord. Amen.

[*The service leader walks to locations of the care recipient's personal possessions.*]

[Name], you and [name of family members] have carefully chosen personal items to bring with you to your new home. These treasured items have cherished memories associated with them. We read from Luke 12:34, "For where your treasure is, there your heart will be also" (NRSV). Let us pray. O God, your gifts to us are many. Bless the cherished keepsakes that [name] has brought with her (him) to her (his) new home. May the memories associated with them be a source of strength, comfort, and blessing; through Jesus Christ our Lord. And help us all to remember the true treasure we have in you, Lord Jesus. Amen.

Communion may be served. Some families may not have received Communion together recently.

The Lord's Prayer
Our Father, who art in heaven, hallowed be thy name, thy kingdom come, thy will be done, on earth as it is in heaven. Give us this day our daily bread; and forgive us our trespasses, as we forgive those who trespass against us; and lead us not into temptation, but deliver us from evil. For thine is the kingdom, and the power, and the glory, forever and ever. Amen.

Recorded Hymn: "Bless This House"

Benediction:
The Lord bless you and keep you. The Lord make his face shine upon you and be gracious to you. The Lord look upon you with favor and give you peace. In the name of the Father, Son, and Holy Spirit. Amen.[1]

Appendix D: Spiritual Journey Exercise for Individuals[1]

The primary purpose of the Spiritual Journey Exercise is to help individuals to reflect on their faith journeys. As they do so, they develop an understanding of how God has been with them in the past, is with them in the present, and will continue to be with them in the future, providing strength, meaning, and peace. Caregivers are encouraged to use any of the following reflection questions that are relevant to their care recipient's life situation. Used as a whole, this exercise can be the care recipient's spiritual legacy. Some care recipients may want to speak their answers into a tape recorder or video recorder.

I. *Church Background*
   A. What congregations have you been affiliated with?
   B. Did you notice any differences in their beliefs and practices?
   C. What do you appreciate most about your current congregational affiliation?

II. *Worship*
   A. How often did you attend worship during your childhood and youth, young adulthood, mature adulthood, and the past two years?
   B. If you did not attend regularly, what were the reasons?
      1. Transportation limitations
      2. Weather
      3. Structural factors at the church (for example, too many steps, heavy doors, no elevator)
      4. Physical limitations
      5. Psychological or spiritual challenges (possibly including anger at the pastor, the congregation, or God)

      6. Lack of interest

      7. Other

  C. Do you listen to Christian radio broadcasts? If so, which ones, and what meaning do they have for you?

  D. Do you watch Christian television programs? If so, which ones? How are they meaningful for you?

  E. What are some of your favorite hymns or worship songs? How are they meaningful for you?

  F. In which church groups or activities were or are you active?

_____

_____

_____

_____

III. *Scripture*

  A. What are your favorite Bible passages and stories? What special meaning do they have for you?

_____

_____

_____

_____

  B. What are your favorite parts of the Bible? Why are they favorites?

  C. How often do you read the Bible?

  D. Do you read daily devotional books and other spiritual literature? If so, which ones? How are they meaningful for you?

IV. *Prayer*

  A. What are your preferred forms of prayer?

      1. Personal free-flowing prayer

      2. Prayers during worship services

      3. Memorized bedtime prayer

       4. Music: hymns, choral, instrumental

       5. The Lord's Prayer

       6. Table grace

       7. Silent prayer

       8. Printed prayers

       9. Other

    B. For what do you pray?

    C. How often do you pray?

       1. All day

       2. Several times a day

       3. Once a day

       4. Only in an emergency or crisis

       5. Never

V. *Baptism and Communion*

    A. If you have been baptized, how old were you?

    B. What was your parents' or your denomination when you were baptized?

    C. What have you been told about your baptism, or what do you remember?

       1. Where were you baptized?

       2. Where did you live at the time?

       3. Did you have sponsors?

       4. Did you wear a special baptismal gown?

    D. What does it mean to you that you have been baptized?

    E. Have there been especially significant baptisms in your family or among your friends? What made them significant?

    F. When and where did you receive your first Communion?

    G. What does Communion mean to you?

    H. How often do you like to receive Communion?

VI. *God*

    A. How do you view God? As a God of:

       1. Love and mercy

       2. Anger and judgment

       3. Distance and hiddenness

       4. Peace and joy

5. Promise and hope

6. Control

B. What role has God had throughout your life?

C. How is your relationship with God?

   1. Close and personal

   2. Occasional, in which you turn to God once in a while

   3. Nonexistent

D. Do you sometimes become angry with God? If so, when? How do you feel about being angry with God?

E. How do you serve God in your life?

VII. *Jesus*

A. Who is Jesus to you?

   1. Friend

   2. Comforter

   3. Shepherd

   4. Savior

   5. Teacher

   6. Other

B. To what extent is Jesus a source of comfort and strength for you?

   1. A great deal

   2. Quite a bit

   3. Some

   4. Not at all

C. Do you believe that God forgives your sins through Jesus' death and resurrection?

D. Do you have past or current sins that trouble you?

   1. If so, would you like to talk about them with the pastor?

VIII. *Meaning*

A. What were the most meaningful religious events and spiritual experiences in your childhood? What meaning did the have for you?

B. What have been the most meaningful religious events and spiritual experiences in your adulthood? What meaning did they have for you?

C. Do you have a reason to get up each morning? If so, what is it?

D. How has the meaning of your life changed over the years?

E. Does your faith give meaning to your life? If so, how?

F. What is your philosophy of life?

G. Do you find meaning in illness, stress, and affliction? If so, what have you found?

H. How do you cope with illness, stress, and affliction?
   1. Become depressed
   2. Give up
   3. Shed tears
   4. Pray laments ("Why me?" "How long?")
   5. Pray for strength and comfort
   6. Trust in God
   7. Seek options
   8. Other

I. Have you experienced meaningful dreams, religious or non-religious? If so, describe a dream and its meaning.

J. How do you meaningfully contribute to the well-being of others?
   1. Volunteer work
   2. Doing good deeds for others
   3. Sharing my creative expertise with others

IX. *Perspective on Aging*

A. What are the best things about your age now?

B. What do you hope for as you grow older?

C. What is the most difficult part of growing old?

D. What do you hope that you never have to give up?

E. What is your secret to living a long life?

X. *Death and Afterlife*

A. Have you had any near-death experiences? If so, describe them and the meaning they had for you.

B. Do you fear death? If so, do you feel comfortable making an appointment with your pastor to talk about your fears?

C. What do you want to do before you die?

D. Is there something important you would like to say to someone before you die? What? Can you tell this person? When?

E. What is your view of the afterlife?

F. If you believe in heaven, what do you look forward to there?

G. As you look ahead to your inevitable death, which of the following would you prefer in your last days?

   1. Family presence
   2. Close friends' presence
   3. Pastoral presence
   4. Being alone
   5. Receiving Communion
   6. Reading Scripture
   7. Recorded music (give examples)

H. Have you completed your "Preplanning Your Funeral or Memorial Service Form"?

I. Have you completed a health care directive and shared it with the appropriate people?

XI. *Christian Decision Making*

A. Does your faith help you make decisions? If so, how?

B. How often do you try to discover what God wants you to do when you have decisions to make?

C. What most strongly influences your decision making?

D. What types of decisions do you allow others to help you make?

E. What types of decisions do you want to make by yourself?

XII. *Peace*

A. How often do you experience inner peace?

B. When do you experience inner peace?

C. If you do not experience inner peace, what hinders you from experiencing it?

XIII. *Faith*

A. What nurtures your faith?

   1. Worship attendance
   2. Bible reading

3. Prayer
4. Pastoral visitation
5. Receiving Communion
6. Devotional reading
7. Talking about faith with other people
8. Religious art and music
9. Other

XIV. *Religious Questions*

A. Do you have religious questions that you would like to discuss?

B. Would you like to call your pastor to make an appointment to discuss your questions?

Appendix E: More Bible Passages for Caregivers

CHAPTER 1: CAREGIVING IS A SPIRITUAL CALLING

- "When the Son of Man comes in his glory, and all the angels with him, he will sit on his throne in heavenly glory. All the nations will be gathered before him, and he will separate the people one from another as a shepherd separates the sheep from the goats. He will put the sheep on his right and the goats on his left. Then the King will say to those on his right, 'Come, you who are blessed by my Father; take your inheritance, the kingdom prepared for you since the creation of the world. For I was hungry and you gave me something to eat, I was thirsty and you gave me something to drink, I was a stranger and you invited me in, I needed clothes and you clothed me, I was sick and you looked after me, I was in prison and you came to visit me.' Then the righteous will answer him, 'Lord, when did we see you hungry and feed you, or thirsty and give you something to drink? When did we see you a stranger and invite you in, or needing clothes and clothe you? When did we see you sick or in prison and go to visit you?' The King will reply, 'I tell you the truth, whatever you did for one of the least of these brothers of mine, you did for me' " (Matthew 25:31–40).

- "On one occasion an expert in the law stood up to test Jesus. 'Teacher,' he asked, 'what must I do to inherit eternal life?' 'What is written in the law?' he replied. 'How do you read it?' He answered, 'Love the Lord your God with all your heart and with all your soul and with all your strength and with all your mind'; and, 'Love your neighbor as yourself.' 'You have answered correctly,' Jesus replied. 'Do this and you will live' " (Luke 10:25–28).

- "But he wanted to justify himself, so he asked Jesus, 'And who is my neighbor?' In reply Jesus said: 'A man was going down from Jerusalem to Jericho, when he fell into the hands of robbers. They stripped him of his clothes, beat him and went away, leaving him half dead. A priest happened to be going down the same road, and when he saw the man, he passed by on the other side. So too, a Levite, when he came to the place and saw him, passed by on the other side. But a Samaritan, as he traveled, came where the man was; and when he saw him, he took pity on him. He went to him and bandaged his wounds, pouring on oil and wine. Then he put the man on his own donkey, took him to an inn and took care of him. The next day he took out two silver coins and gave them to the innkeeper. "Look after him," he said, "and when I return, I will reimburse you for any extra expense you may have." Which of these three do you think was a neighbor to the man who fell into the hands of robbers?' The expert in the law replied, 'The one who had mercy on him.' Jesus told him, 'Go and do likewise' " (Luke 10:29–37).

- Jesus said, "I give you a new commandment, that you love one another. Just as I have loved you, you also should love one another. By this everyone will know that you are my disciples, if you have love for one another" (John 13:34–35 NRSV).

CHAPTER 2: BECOMING AND GROWING AS A CAREGIVER

- "I lift up my eyes to the hills—where does my help come from? My help comes from the Lord, the Maker of heaven and earth. He will not let your foot slip—he who watches over you will not slumber; indeed, he who watches over Israel will neither slumber nor sleep" (Psalm 121:1–4).

- "In everything, do to others what you would have them do to you" (Matthew 7:12).

- "I can do everything through him who gives me strength" (Philippians 4:13).

- "Therefore, as God's chosen people, holy and dearly loved, clothe yourselves with compassion, kindness, humility, gentleness and patience. Bear with each other and forgive whatever grievances you may have against one another. Forgive as the Lord forgave you. And over all these virtues put on love, which binds them all together in perfect unity. Let the peace of Christ rule in your hearts, since as members of one body you were called to peace" (Colossians 3:12–15).

- "God abides in those who confess that Jesus is the Son of God, and they abide in God" (1 John 4:15 NRSV).

CHAPTER 3: SPIRITUAL NURTURE FOR CAREGIVERS

- "When the cares of my heart are many, your consolations cheer my soul" (Psalm 94:19 NRSV).

- "Therefore, since through God's mercy we have this ministry, we do not lose heart" (2 Corinthians 4:1).

- "Consider him who endured such hostility against himself from sinners [Jesus], so that you may not grow weary or lose heart" (Hebrews 12:3 NRSV).

- "Finally, all of you, have unity of spirit, sympathy, love for one another, a tender heart, and a humble mind" (1 Peter 3:8 NRSV).

CHAPTER 4: PSYCHOLOGICAL NURTURE FOR CAREGIVERS

Anger and depression

- "How long, O Lord? Will you forget me forever? How long will you hide your face from me? How long must I wrestle with my thoughts and every day have sorrow in my heart?

How long will my enemy triumph over me? Look on me and answer, O Lord my God. Give light to my eyes, or I will sleep in death; my enemy will say, 'I have overcome him,' and my foes will rejoice when I fall. But I trust in your unfailing love; my heart rejoices in your salvation. I will sing to the Lord, for he has been good to me" (Psalm 13).

- "A gentle answer turns away wrath, but a harsh word stirs up anger" (Proverbs 15:1).

- "Come to me, all you who are weary and burdened, and I will give you rest. Take my yoke upon you and learn from me, for I am gentle and humble in heart, and you will find rest for your souls. For my yoke is easy and my burden is light" (Matthew 11:28–30).

- " 'In your anger do not sin': Do not let the sun go down while you are still angry" (Ephesians 4:26).

Comfort

- "O Lord, you have searched me and you know me. You know when I sit and when I rise; you perceive my thoughts from afar. You discern my going out and my lying down; you are familiar with all my ways. Before a word is on my tongue you know it completely, O Lord. You hem me in—behind and before; you have laid your hand upon me. Such knowledge is too wonderful for me, too lofty for me to attain. Where can I go from your Spirit? Where can I flee from your presence? If I go up to the heavens, you are there; if I make my bed in the depths, you are there. If I rise on the wings of the dawn, if I settle on the far side of the sea, even there your hand will guide me, your right hand will hold me fast. If I say, 'Surely the darkness will hide me and the light become night around me,' even the darkness will not be dark to you; the night will shine like the day, for darkness is as light to you. For you created my inmost being; you knit me together in my mother's womb. I praise you because I am fearfully and wonderfully made; your works are wonderful, I know that full well. My frame was not hidden from you when I was made in the secret place. When I was woven together in the depths of the earth, your eyes saw my unformed body. All the days ordained for me were written in your book before one of them came to be. How precious to me are your thoughts, O God! How vast is the sum of them! Were I to count them, they would outnumber the grains of sand. When I awake, I am still with you. . . . Search me, O God, and know my heart; test me and know my anxious thoughts. See if there is any offensive way in me, and lead me in the way everlasting" (Psalm 139:1–18, 23–24).

- "Praise be to the God and Father of our Lord Jesus Christ, the Father of compassion and the God of all comfort, who comforts us in all our troubles, so that we can comfort those in any trouble with the comfort we ourselves have received from God" (2 Corinthians 1:3–4).

- "May our Lord Jesus Christ himself and God our Father, who loved us and by his grace gave us eternal encouragement and good hope, encourage your hearts and strengthen you in every good deed and word" (2 Thessalonians 2:16–17).

Peace

- " 'Though the mountains be shaken and the hills be removed, yet my unfailing love for you will not be shaken nor my covenant of peace be removed,' says the Lord, who has compassion on you" (Isaiah 54:10).

- "That day when evening came, he said to his disciples, 'Let us go over to the other side.' Leaving the crowd behind, they took him along, just as he was, in the boat. There were also other boats with him. A furious squall came up, and the waves broke over the boat, so that it was nearly swamped. Jesus was in the stern, sleeping on a cushion. The disciples woke him and said to him, 'Teacher, don't you care if we drown?' He got up, rebuked the wind and said to the waves, 'Quiet! Be still!' Then the wind died down and it was completely calm. He said to his disciples, 'Why are you so afraid? Do you still have no faith?' They were terrified and asked each other, 'Who is this? Even the wind and the waves obey him!' " (Mark 4:35–41).

- "[Jesus] said to them, 'Come with me by yourselves to a quiet place and get some rest' " (Mark 6:31).

- "Do not be anxious about anything, but in everything, by prayer and petition, with thanksgiving, present your requests to God. And the peace of God, which transcends all understanding, will guard your hearts and your minds in Christ Jesus" (Philippians 4:6–7).

CHAPTER 5: BASIC CAREGIVING TIPS

- "Therefore we do not lose heart. Though outwardly we are wasting away, yet inwardly we are being renewed day by day" (2 Corinthians 4:16).

- "As a prisoner for the Lord, then, I urge you to live a life worthy of the calling you have received. Be completely humble and gentle; be patient, bearing with one another in love. Make every effort to keep the unity of the Spirit through the bond of peace" (Ephesians 4:1–3).

- "Everyone should be quick to listen, slow to speak and slow to become angry" (James 1:19).

- "If anyone speaks, he should do it as one speaking the very words of God. If anyone serves, he should do it with the strength God provides, so that in all things God may be praised through Jesus Christ. To him be the glory and the power for ever and ever. Amen" (1 Peter 4:11).

CHAPTER 6: HELPFUL EQUIPMENT AND PROFESSIONAL HOME HEALTH CARE

- "The Lord bless you and keep you; the Lord make his face

shine upon you and be gracious to you; the Lord turn his face toward you and give you peace" (Numbers 6:24–26).

- "Be strong and courageous. Do not be terrified; do not be discouraged, for the Lord your God will be with you wherever you go" (Joshua 1:9).

- "I have come that they may have life, and have it to the full" (John 10:10).

- "And I will ask the Father, and he will give you another Counselor to be with you forever" (John 14:16).

CHAPTER 7: CARING FOR PARENTS

- "God is our refuge and strength, an ever-present help in trouble. Therefore we will not fear, though the earth give way and the mountains fall into the heart of the sea, though its waters roar and foam and the mountains quake with their surging. There is a river whose streams make glad the city of God, the holy place where the Most High dwells. God is within her, she will not fall; God will help her at break of day. Nations are in uproar, king-doms fall; he lifts his voice, the earth melts. The Lord Almighty is with us; the God of Jacob is our fortress. . . . 'Be still, and know that I am God; I will be exalted among the nations, I will be exalted in the earth.' The Lord Almighty is with us; the God of Jacob is our fortress" (Psalm 46:1–7, 10–11).

- "And [Jesus] will answer them, 'Truly I tell you, just as you did it to one of the least of these who are members of my family, you did it to me' " (Matthew 25:40 NRSV).

- "May the God of hope fill you with all joy and peace as you trust in him, so that you may overflow with hope by the power of the Holy Spirit" (Romans 15:13).

- "Finally . . . whatever is true, whatever is noble, whatever is right, whatever is pure, whatever is lovely, whatever is admi-rable—if anything is excellent or praiseworthy—think about such things. Whatever you have learned or received or heard from me, or seen in me—put it into practice. And the God of peace will be with you" (Philippians 4:8–9).

CHAPTER 8: CARING FOR YOUR SPOUSE

- "The Lord himself goes before you and will be with you; he will never leave you nor forsake you. Do not be afraid; do not be discouraged" (Deuteronomy 31:8).

- "Be strong and take heart, all you who hope in the Lord" (Psalm 31:24).

- "As the deer pants for streams of water, so my soul pants for you, O God" (Psalm 42:1).

- "So do not fear, for I am with you; do not be dismayed, for I am your God. I will strengthen you and help you; I will uphold you with my righteous right hand" (Isaiah 41:10).

- "Then he got into the boat and his disciples followed him. Without warning, a furious storm came up on the lake, so that the waves swept over the boat. But Jesus was sleeping. The disciples went and woke him, saying, 'Lord, save us! We're going to drown!' He replied, 'You of little faith, why are you so afraid?' Then he got up and rebuked the winds and the waves, and it was completely calm. The men were amazed and asked, 'What kind of man is this? Even the winds and the waves obey him!' " (Matthew 8:23–27).

CHAPTER 9: LONG-DISTANCE CAREGIVING

- "Those of steadfast mind you keep in peace—in peace because they trust in you. Trust in the Lord for ever, for in the Lord God you have an everlasting rock" (Isaiah 26:3–4 NRSV).

- "Comfort, comfort my people, says your God" (Isaiah 40:1).

- "Then Jesus told them a parable about their need to pray always and not to lose heart" (Luke 18:1 NRSV).

- "Do everything in love" (1 Corinthians 16:14).

CHAPTER 10: CELEBRATING HOLIDAYS AND BIRTHDAYS

- "How precious is your steadfast love, O God! All people may take refuge in the shadow of your wings" (Psalm 36:7 NRSV).

- "Come, let us sing for joy to the Lord; let us shout aloud to the Rock of our salvation. Let us come before him with thanksgiving and extol him with music and song. For the Lord is a great God, the great King above all gods. In his hand are the depths of the earth, and the mountain peaks belong to him. The sea is his, for he made it, and his hands formed the dry land. Come, let us bow down in worship, let us kneel before the Lord our Maker; for he is our God and we are the people of his pasture, the flock under his care" (Psalm 95:1–7).

- "Praise the Lord, O my soul; all my inmost being, praise his holy name. Praise the Lord, O my soul, and forget not all his benefits—who forgives all your sins and heals all your diseases, who redeems your life from the pit and crowns you with love and compassion, who satisfies your desires with good things so that your youth is renewed like the eagle's. . . . For as high as the heavens are above the earth, so great is his love for those who fear him; as far as the east is from the west, so far has he removed our transgressions from us. As a father has compassion on his children, so the Lord has compassion on those who fear him. . . . The Lord has established his throne in heaven, and his kingdom rules over all. Praise the Lord, you his angels, you mighty ones who do his bidding, who obey his word. Praise the Lord, all his heavenly hosts, you his servants who do his will. Praise the Lord, all his works everywhere in his dominion. Praise the Lord, O my soul" (Psalm 103:1–5, 11–13, 19–22).

- "Yet this I call to mind and therefore I have hope: Because of the Lord's great love we are not consumed, for his compassions never fail. They are new every morning; great is your faithfulness. I say to myself, 'The Lord is my portion; therefore I will wait for him.' The Lord is good to those whose hope is in him, to the one who seeks him" (Lamentations 3:21–25).

CHAPTER 11: NURSING HOMES, ASSISTED-LIVING FACILITIES, AND OTHER CARE FACILITIES

- "To you, O Lord, I lift up my soul; in you I trust, O my God" (Psalm 25:1–2).
- "When I am afraid, I will trust in you" (Psalm 56:3).
- "For God all things are possible" (Mark 10:27 NRSV).
- "When Jesus spoke again to the people, he said, 'I am the light of the world. Whoever follows me will never walk in darkness, but will have the light of life' " (John 8:12).

CHAPTER 12: DEALING WITH YOUR LOVED ONE'S DYING AND DEATH PROCESS

- "Martha said to Jesus, 'Lord, if you had been here, my brother would not have died. But even now I know that God will give you whatever you ask of him.' Jesus said to her, 'Your brother will rise again.' Martha said to him, 'I know that he will rise again in the resurrection on the last day.' Jesus said to her, 'I am the resurrection and the life. Those who believe in me, even though they die, will live, and everyone who lives and believes in me will never die' " (John 11:21–26 NRSV).
- "[Nothing] will be able to separate us from the love of God in Christ Jesus" (Romans 8:39 NRSV).
- "After that, we who are still alive and are left will be caught up together with them in the clouds to meet the Lord in the air. And so we will be with the Lord forever" (1 Thessalonians 4:17).

CHAPTER 13: COMFORT AND SUPPORT IN YOUR BEREAVEMENT

- "The Lord is close to the brokenhearted and saves those who are crushed in spirit" (Psalm 34:18).

- "Do not be afraid, little flock, for your Father has been pleased to give you the kingdom" (Luke 12:32).

- " 'Do not let your hearts be troubled. Trust in God; trust also in me. In my Father's house are many rooms; if it were not so, I would have told you. I am going there to prepare a place for you. And if I go and prepare a place for you, I will come back and take you to be with me that you also may be where I am. You know the way to the place where I am going.' Thomas said to him, 'Lord, we don't know where you are going, so how can we know the way?' Jesus answered, 'I am the way and the truth and the life. No one comes to the Father except through me' " (John 14:1–6).

- "Praise be to the God and Father of our Lord Jesus Christ! In his great mercy he has given us a new birth into a living hope through the resurrection of Jesus Christ from the dead" (1 Peter 1:3).

Appendix F: Caregiving Web Sites

GOVERNMENT SITES

Medical Benefits Checkup
www.benefitscheckup.org
This easy-to-use benefits checkup will quickly tell you if your care recipient qualifies for government-sponsored benefits and programs in her geographical area.

Medicare
www.medicare.gov
This site posts inspection results for nursing homes in the United States. Do not neglect to use this site when evaluating and selecting a nursing home. This site is also a Medicare information clearing house.

OSHA (Occupational Safety and Health Administration)
www.osha.gov
This site includes government-required safety and health regulations that health care facilities are required to follow, as well as procedures to follow when you want to report a possible negligent facility.

Social Security Administration
www.ssa.gov

United States Administration on Aging
www.aoa.gov
This official federal agency is dedicated to policy development, planning, and the delivery of supportive home- and community-based services to older persons and their caregivers.

United States Department of Veterans Affairs
★www.va.gov

United States National Library of Medicine and the National Institutes of Health
★www.medlineplus.gov
This site provides trusted health information.

NATIONAL ORGANIZATION SITES

American Society on Aging
★www.asaging.org

Assisted Living Federation of America
★www.alfa.org

Families USA—The Voice for Health Care Consumers
★www.familiesusa.org

Family Caregiver Alliance, National Center on Caregiving
★www.caregiver.org
This site provides support to family caregivers and personalized assistance in locating community resources and services, as well as publications on caregiving issues.

Hospice Association of America
★www.hospice-america.org

National Academy of Elder Law Attorneys
★www.naela.org

National Association of Area Agencies on Aging
★www.n4a.org
This site puts you in touch with your geographical agency that can answer most of your questions.

National Association for Home Care
★www.nahc.org

This site provides information on home and hospice care, including details for finding outside home care.

National Association of Professional Geriatric Care Managers
www.caremanager.org

National Council on Aging
www.ncoa.org

National Family Caregivers Association
www.thefamilycaregiver.org
This organization provides caregiving newsletters, a family caregiver support program, a prescription drug discount program, greeting cards for caregivers, bereavement kits, and an opportunity to participate in caregiver research.

National Partnership for Women and Families
www.nationalpartnership.org
This nonprofit and nonpartisan site promotes fairness in the workplace, quality health care, and policies that help women and men meet the dual demands of work and family. It also provides detailed information about the National Family and Medical Leave Act.

National Respite Locator Service
www.respitelocator.org

OTHER CAREGIVING SITES

Advocating Quality End-of-Life Care
www.Partnershipforcaring.org
This site includes information and health care directives for all states.

The Caregiver's Home Companion
www.caregivershome.com
This site features many types of caregiving and a weekly e-mail newsletter that is packed with important news affecting caregivers and the elderly.

Children of Aging Parents
www.caps4caregivers.org
A nonprofit, charitable organization whose mission is to assist the nation's caregivers of the elderly or chronically ill.

Eden Alternative
www.edenalt.com
This site provides the newest philosophy in long-term care. It is the up-and-coming form of supervised care for the elderly. It also includes locations of current Eden Alternative homes, as well as information about the Green House Project. Dr. Bill Thomas founded this movement in 1991.

ElderCare Online Internet Community
www.ec-online.net
This site includes "caregiver chat" and "chat with professionals," as well as a bimonthly newsletter.

Empowering Caregivers
www.care-givers.com
This site includes caregiving articles, chat, message boards, forums, newsletters, etc.

MEDICAL SITES

Alzheimer's Association
www.alz.org

Alzheimer's Disease Education and Referral Center
www.alzheimers.org

American Arthritis Foundation
www.arthritis.org

American Cancer Society
www.cancer.org

American Diabetes Association
www.diabetes.org

American Heart Association
www.americanheart.org

Brain Injury Association of America
www.biausa.org

Cancer Care
www.cancercare.org
Cancer Care is a nonprofit organization whose mission is to provide free professional help to people with all types of cancers through counseling, education, information and referral, and direct financial assistance.

National Alliance on Mental Illness
www.nami.org

National Institute of Neurological Disorders and Stroke
www.ninds.nih.gov

Endnotes

Chapter 1: Caregiving Is a Spiritual Calling

1. I. Howard Marshall, *The Gospel of Luke: A Commentary on the Greek Text* (Grand Rapids, MI: William B. Eerdmans Publishing Company, 1979), 445.

2. C. S. Mann, *Mark: A New Translation. The Anchor Bible.* (Garden City, New York: Doubleday & Company, Inc., 1986), 481.

3. Gerhard Kittel, ed., with Geoffrey W. Bromily, trans. and ed., *Theological Dictionary of the New Testament, Volume I* (Grand Rapids, MI: William B. Eerdmans Publishing Company, 1964), 46.

Chapter 2: Becoming and Growing As a Caregiver

1. National Family Caregivers Association Random Survey of 1,000 Adults, Summer 2000, *www.nfcacares.org/who_are_family_caregivers/care_giving_statistics.cfm*.

2. Ibid.

3. Bernice L. Neugarten, "The Young-Old and the Age-Irrelevant Society." Lecture for the Couchiching Institute on Public Affairs, Toronto, Canada, February 1979, 1–6.

4. Dr. Rhonda Montgomery, "Care for Caregivers: Reaching Out for Help." Lecture, Third International Conference on Family Caregiving, Washington, D.C., October 14, 2002.

5. "Caregiving in the U.S.," National Alliance for Caregiving and American Association of Retired Persons, April 2004, 32.

6. Ibid., 66.

Chapter 3: Spiritual Nurture for Caregivers

1. Lois D. Knutson, *Understanding the Senior Adult: A Tool for Wholistic Ministry* (Bethesda, MD: The Alban Institute, 1999), 176–83.

Chapter 4: Psychological Nurture for Caregivers

1. Nighttime challenges may include regular telephone calls from your loved one who lives by himself or frequent awakenings to help your care recipient (who lives with you) to and in the bathroom, or to dispense medications and perform medical procedures (such as changing oxygen tanks), comfort a wandering or depressed care recipient, or turn your loved one in bed to prevent pressure sores.

2. This machine helps you fall asleep to the sound of rainfall, ocean waves, white noise, etc. They can be purchased from *www.timeformecatalog.com* and many retail stores.

Chapter 5: Basic Caregiving Tips

1. Remember that you are not the cause of this behavior. Your loved one may have been this way all his life, may be totally frustrated with his loss of independence and identity, and may express his frustrations in inappropriate ways. Lower your expectations to successfully reason with (or cure) a loved one who behaves like this. Arguing or becoming defensive will not work. The best approach is to listen and reflect back your loved one's feelings. As you attempt to understand how he developed this personality trait, you will respond to him more compassionately.

2. The following tips may help you address this situation: (1) Prior to bringing up this subject, research local alternatives, e.g., senior transportation services, disability services, and businesses that provide home delivery (such as pharmacies and supermarkets). Remember that losing one's driver's license leads to feelings of isolation and depression. (2) Try to convince your loved one of the wisdom of reducing his driving radius, amount of driving, and time for driving to the least congested hours of the day. Affirm his safe driving record (if he has one) and encourage him to keep it that way. (3) If he insists upon driving, provide documentation of accident reports, other people's complaints, and your observations. (4) Mechanically alter the vehicle so that it cannot be driven. This strategy will not successfully deter him, however, if he is capable of calling a mechanic to come and repair the vehicle. (5) Make an appointment with the family physician and advise him of the situation in advance of the appointment. Ask the doctor to evaluate your loved one's ability to drive. (6) Make an appointment with an ophthalmologist to ascertain

whether your loved one sees adequately to drive. Good vision, however, does not address the cognitive concern of your loved one's becoming lost while driving. (7) Suggest that your loved one have the Department of Motor Vehicles retest his eyes, on-road driving ability, and knowledge of traffic laws. (8) If your loved one refuses these suggestions, report him to the Department of Motor Vehicles. Outside parties take the onus off you, thereby helping you to maintain your positive relationship with your loved one.

3. Anger may be expressed through frequent complaints (about food quality, weather, too little or too much exercise, home health care workers, etc.) and unwillingness to cooperate with you or other caregivers. Anger may be caused by her losses in life and dependent life situation.

4. In addition to dementia, confusion may be caused by stress, lack of knowledge regarding her medical situation, apprehension about making decisions, shortness of breath, pain, or medications.

5. This may be caused by dry mouth, shortness of breath, or medications. Teeth, dentures, or partials may need attention from a dentist.

6. You may also want to purchase a special computer that is made for those who are unable to speak.

7. Directions for hand massage given by Pat Haga, certified massage therapist, at the "Eighth Summer Institute on Geriatrics: Dementia, Quality of Life, Falls," University of Minnesota, June 1998, Minneapolis, MN.

8. Directions for foot massage are given by Heather S. Richardson, Forester Salon, Inc., Forest City, IA, October 15, 2004.

Chapter 6: Helpful Equipment and Professional Home Health Care

1. "Coming Next: Wireless Healthcare on Your Cell Phone," *The Caregiver's Home Companion,* November 1, 2005, *www.caregivershome.com/news/article. cfm?UID=739.*

2. "Make Way for Carebots—the Newest Caregiver?" *The Caregiver's Home Companion,* October 4, 2005, *www.caregivershome.com/news/article. cfm?UID=716.*

3. "Study Finds Long-Term Care Needs Go Unmet," *Caregivers USA News—And Thou Shalt Honor,* Vol. II, No. 17, April 5, 2004, 1.

Chapter 7: Caring for Parents

1. "Workplace Flexibility: Balancing Work and Caregiving," American Association of Retired Persons, *www.aarp.org/money/careers/flexiblework/a2003-10-27-caregiving-balancingwork.html*.

2. "Family Leave Benefits Would Help Caregivers Put Their Families First," National Partnership for Women and Families, November 1, 2004, *www.nationalpartnership.org/portals/p3/library/WorkplaceFlexibility/WhyCaregiversNeedFamilyLeaveBenefits.pdf*.

3. Belden, Russonello, and Stewart, "In the Middle: A Report on Multicultural Boomers Coping With Family and Aging Issues," American Association of Retired Persons, July 2001, *www.aarp.org/research/housing-mobility/caregiving/aresearch-import-789-D17446.html*.

4. "Sixty-five Plus in the United States," U.S. Census Bureau, pp. 10, 58, *www.census.gov/prod/1/pop/p23-190/p23-190.pdf*.

5. "Hearing Loss," National Institute on Aging, Age Page, *www.nia publications.org/agepages/hearing.asp*.

6. P. F. Adams and M. A. Marano, "Current Estimates From the National Health Interview Survey, 1994," *National Center for Health Statistics Vital Health Statistics* 10, No. 2193 (1995): 83–4.

7. Ibid.

8. Patricia Beard, *Good Daughters: Loving Our Mothers as They Age* (New York, Warner Books, 1999), 63.

9. Ibid.

10. Ibid.

11. Ibid.

12. Ibid., 64.

13. "Among family caregivers who participated in a 2001 survey conducted by The Caregivers Advisory Panel, almost 80 percent reported that they were the primary purchasers of health products. More than half purchased incontinence products, specialty bathing and skin care supplies, and nutritional supplements. More than a third bought wound care or wound prevention products, while more than one-fourth of family caregivers provided home safety accessories. A family involved in caregiving can, for example, expect to spend approximately $1,500 annually for incontinence products and as much as $2 a day on nutritional supplements. The

1997 NAC/AARP survey of caregivers found that those who paid out of pocket for needed products or services spent an average of $171 per month; a total estimate of $1.5 billion per month was spent on a national basis by all caregivers. For the approximately 6.7 million long-distance caregivers, who live at least an hour away from the care recipient, the costs can be even higher." Source: "The Economic Impact of Family Caregiving," Donna L. Wagner and Paul Alper, *And Thou Shalt Honor Viewers Guide* (Culver City, CA: Wiland-Bell Productions and Barksdale Ballard & Company, 2002), 11.

14. "A Painful Source of Marital Strife: When an Elderly Parent Moves In," Sue Shellenbarger, *Wall Street Journal*, New York, NY, April 1, 2004, D1.

Chapter 8: Caring for Your Spouse

1. "Rabbi Ben Ezra," Robert Browning, *www.poeticexpressions.co.uk/POEMS/Grow%20old%20along%20with%20me*.

2. "Selected Caregiver Statistics," The Family Caregiver Alliance National Center on Caregiving, *www.caregiver.org/caregiver/jsp/content_node.jsp?nodeid=439*.

3. "Caregiving Statistics—Statistics on Family Caregivers and Family Caregiving," National Family Caregivers Association, *www.thefamilycaregiver.org/who/stats.cfm#3*.

4. "Selected Caregiver Statistics."

Chapter 9: Long-Distance Caregiving

1. "Long-Distance Love Is a Costly Affair—Caregiving From Afar," The Caregiver's Home Companion Web site, *www.caregivershome.com/news/article.cfm?UID=91,* posted August 30, 2004.

2. Judith Delaney and Teresa Dodson, "Long-Distance Caregiving: Experience of a Multiyear Demonstrated Project," lecture, American Society on Aging and National Council on Aging National Convention, New Orleans, LA, March 8, 2001.

3. Ibid.

4. "Long-Distance Love Is a Costly Affair."

5. Ibid.

6. Ibid.

Chapter 11: Nursing Homes, Assisted-Living Facilities, and Other Care Facilities

1. Beth Witrogen McLeod and Theodore Roszak, "America Needs a Caregiver Corps," *Aging Today,* the newsletter of the American Society on Aging, San Francisco, CA, January/February 2001, 12.

2. Lois D. Knutson, *Understanding the Senior Adult: A Tool for Wholistic Ministry* (Bethesda, MD: The Alban Institute, 1999), 123–25.

Chapter 12: Dealing With Your Loved One's Dying and Death Process

1. Michael Rybarski, "Rewriting the Rules: How Boomers Will Deal With Death," *Aging Today* (newsletter of the American Society on Aging, San Francisco, CA), September-October 2004, 12.

2. Johann Christoph Arnold, *Be Not Afraid* (Farmington, PA: The Plough Publishing House, 1996), 170.

Chapter 13: Comfort and Support in Your Bereavement

1. Washington Irving, "Washington Irving Quotes," Thinkexist.com, September 12, 2006, *thinkexist.com/quotation/there_is_a_sacredness_in_tears-they_are_not_the/149959.html.*

2. Lois D. Knutson, *Understanding the Senior Adult: A Tool for Wholistic Ministry* (Bethesda, MD: The Alban Institute, 1999), 164–65.

3. *Lutheran Book of Worship* (Minneapolis and Philadelphia: Augsburg Publishing House and Board of Publication, Lutheran Church in America, 1978), 137.

Appendix C: Blessing of the New Home Service

1. This material has been adapted from *Understanding the Senior Adult: A Tool for Wholistic Ministry* by Lois D. Knutson, with permission from the Alban Institute. Copyright © 1999 by The Alban Institute, Inc., Herndon, VA. All rights reserved.

Appendix D: Spiritual Journey Exercise for Individuals

1. This material has been adapted from *Understanding the Senior Adult: A Tool for Wholistic Ministry* by Lois D. Knutson, with permission from the Alban Institute. Copyright © 1999 by The Alban Institute, Inc., Herndon, VA. All rights reserved.